Drink *the* Pacific Northwest

Neil Ratliff

Drink *the* Pacific Northwest

13-Digit ISBN: 978-1-64643-458-9
10-Digit ISBN: 1-64643-458-7

This book may be ordered by mail from the publisher. Please include $5.99 for postage and handling. Please support your local bookseller first!

Books published by Cider Mill Press Book Publishers are available at special discounts for bulk purchases in the United States by corporations, institutions, and other organizations. For more information, please contact the publisher.

Cider Mill Press Book Publishers
"Where good books are ready for press"
501 Nelson Place
Nashville, Tennessee 37214
cidermillpress.com

Typography: Kepler Standard, Futura PT

Printed in Malaysia
24 25 26 27 28 OFF 5 4 3 2 1
First Edition

Drink *the* Pacific Northwest

The Ultimate Guide to Breweries, Distilleries, Wineries, and Cideries in the Pacific Northwest

Neil Ratliff

CIDER MILL PRESS

BOOK PUBLISHERS

CONTENTS

INTRODUCTION

---

*They said that timing was everything/made him want to
be everywhere/there's a lot to be said for nowhere.*
— Eddie Vedder

Sasquatch is probably not real—but, if the prospect of a hulking hominid
stalking our mountain ranges discourages anyone else from moving here to
the Pacific Northwest, then call me a believer.

That's a joke, of course, a common trope among the wet and bearded inhabitants of Oregon, Washington, Idaho, and British Columbia. It feels like we live in
a secret, forested paradise, and we're all full out here—no more people, please.
Most Easterners think it rains every day in these parts, that we stare at our shoes
in silence waiting in line for coffee, and that we prefer our cocktails not shaken,
but Molotov. If that imagery prevents our rent from being raised and our roads
occupied with one more automobile, then so be it. When Bigfoot scans for vic-
tims, it can tell if you're a Johnny Come Lately, ya know. But at the risk of opening
the gates and inviting a caravan of newcomers into our private slice of heaven,
let me be the one to tell you:

West Coast = Best Coast.

The booze out here is top notch—because we grow what goes into it. We
have the best apples, nearly all of the hops, and the tastiest grapes this side of
the Mississippi. Enjoy IPAs? You're welcome. Like pinot noir? Please, no more
applause. Rejoice with gin? We graciously accept this award on behalf of all junipers. We will even make vodka with the best potatoes in the world while we're at
it. We were just getting started when Prohibition hit, but we took the punches in
stride and we're coming out swinging in this round. The PNW is all about craftsmanship, innovation, and pride—nowhere more apparent than in our wineries,
distilleries, cideries, and breweries.

"Here in the corner attic of America," wrote Timothy Egan in his book *The
Good Rain: Across Time and Terrain in the Pacific Northwest*, "two hours' drive
from a rainforest, a desert, a foreign country, an empty island, a hidden fjord,
a raging river, a glacier, and a volcano is a place where the inhabitants sense
they can do no better, nor do they want to." The geography here truly is unique.

The Cascade Mountain range bifurcates us into two distinct regions: cool, wet, and lush on the left; sunny, dry, and warm on the right—each side with its own climate and therefore its own agriculture. The Yakima Valley is underappreciated for its "breadbasket of America" status, supplying most of the nation's hops, apples, and blueberries. The Columbia River Basin yields wheat and barley by the ton. The supremacy of Idaho's potatoes is unquestioned. Sure, we are centuries overdue for "The Big One," but earthquakes are brief and if nature wants to shake our apple trees for us, we'll take the help, right?

For the booze traveler, the alcohol archaeologist, the sightseer of spirits, I implore you to drive westward and discover what we are doing out here. Lewis and Clark were on to something. Boise is a superb place to begin; overlooked for too long, it has experienced a boom like no other, a gathering of alcohol craftspeople displaced by the rising rents and claustrophobia of California and Colorado. After drinking your fill of Telaya wine and Lost Grove beer, head due north to Coeur D'Alene (call it "CDA" if you want to fit in), stopping to wet your whistle in Lewiston and Moscow. Hook a left to sip vodka at Dry Fly Distillery and continue westward to experience the Yakima Valley, with its endless miles of award-winning vineyards along its sunny slopes. Crank the Pearl Jam playlist as you cruise over the Cascades into Seattle and post up at some of the most inviting, first-class breweries in the country like Fremont and Georgetown, or grab a bottle of tequila (yes, tequila!) at Black Rock Spirits, or try the famous whiskey of OOLA Distillery. Head north to explore Vancouver's thriving beer neighborhoods like Yeast Van and Brewery Creek. Shake off the hangover and head due south toward Portland's flourishing market of craft spirit makers like Wild Roots and Aria to see what these junipers are all about. Make sure to keep going down to Eugene—ColdFire and Ninkasi will have flights of tasty brews made from unparalleled local ingredients. Oh, and don't forget about Bend and the legendary Deschutes brewery, too.

PACIFIC NORTHWEST PRODUCE

—

Good farmers, who take seriously their duties as stewards of Creation and of their land's inheritors, contribute to the welfare of society in more ways than society usually acknowledges, or even knows. These farmers produce valuable goods, of course; but they also conserve soil, they conserve water, they conserve wildlife, they conserve open space, they conserve scenery.
—Wendell Berry, *Bringing It to the Table: On Farming and Food*

There are *a lot* of inputs and processes required to get a glass of booze in your hand. Farmers clear land, plant crops, tend to crops, pray for good weather, harvest crops, and ship crops. Brewers buy malt, hops, barley, grains, and fruits, add (*a lot*) of water, and heat, and apply their magic. Winemakers source grapes from near and far and fill warehouses with barrels. Distillers use myriad plants (and water and heat, *a lot of them*) to spirit our spirits. After that, they all have to bottle, can, and keg the results of their hard work and ship it to our favorite watering holes and stores. The practice of using resources smartly in ways that do not compromise that ability in the future is known as sustainability.

Sustainable practices are undoubtedly good for marketing but more importantly, they are good for everyone's welfare, and for each producer's bottom line, too. When an operation can utilize fewer inputs without sacrificing quality, they save money, and reducing the need for materials translates into a smaller impact on the biosphere. During my travels for this book, I was surprised not only by the innovations I witnessed, but also by their ubiquity, and by the prevalence of these values in the craft beer, wine, and spirits industries. One vineyard dedicates a portion of its land to growing hay, which it trades to the next-door animal preserve for its animals' manure. Distillers who in the past paid astronomical water bills have discovered that simple reclamation systems drastically lower their water needs. A winery in Idaho implemented an ozone cleaning system that sanitizes equipment more effectively while eliminating the use of chemicals. These businesses sell more of their product to a public increasingly concerned with protecting biodiversity and natural resources, but above all, *it's simply the right thing to do.*

Biodynamic Agriculture

—

"BIODYNAMIC AGRICULTURE TREATS THE FARM like a living organism, self-contained and self-sustainable," says Elizabeth Candelario, director of Demeter USA, the nonprofit certifier of biodynamic farms and consumer products in the U.S. (and owner of the trademarked term). The Biodynamic Association defines the practice as a "holistic, ecological, and ethical approach to farming, gardening, food, and nutrition." Essentially, it advocates for agriculture to source its own growing energy via manure and compost, eschewing synthetic fertilizers, pesticides, and herbicides, setting aside a portion of every agricultural operation for the preservation of biodiversity and crop rotation. The process is based on the work of philosopher and scientist Dr. Rudolf Steiner, and some argue that the practice is only philosophical, unable to be tested scientifically. But the multitude of attendees celebrating its centennial anniversary at the yearly Biodynamic Conference might disagree.

APPLES

—

At the turn of the 19th century, American settlers came to the Washington area, the traditional gathering grounds and reservation lands of the Colville Tribes and Yakama Nation tribal people. By 1826, early settlers learned that the area's rich lava-ash soil and plentiful sunshine created ideal conditions for growing apples. The arid climate also meant fewer insect and disease problems, thereby increasing the overall pristine quality of the apples through to harvest. Noting the health and vigor of apple trees planted along stream banks, pioneers developed irrigation systems. By 1889, commercial orchards were established.
—Washington Apple Commission

- Washington State is the top apple producer in the United States. In 2021, it supplied 70 percent of the nation's apples (and 90 percent of all organically grown apples).

- Oregon is the seventh-largest grower of apples.

- The value of the entire apple crop of the Pacific Northwest is over $2 billion per year.

- There are nearly 180,000 acres of apple orchards in the PNW.

- Washington is also the largest producer of sweet cherries, pears, and blueberries.

- There are 7,500 known varieties of apples.

- Frosty winters, supply chain issues, and labor shortages affect apple supply.

- Apples float because they are 85 percent water.

- The science of growing apples is known as pomology.

- Archaeological evidence shows that humans have been eating apples for over 8,000 years.

- All apples are picked by hand, requiring over 40,000 harvest workers in Washington state alone.

Cider

———

"When it reached the land that would be called Washington, the apple knew."
–Tieton Cider Works

"CIDER IS ARGUABLY THE DRINK THAT BUILT THIS NATION," declares *Washington State Magazine*. Cider presses were omnipresent in the homes of colonial Americans, as cider was regarded as safer to consume than water. Before they became agricultural staples of the Pacific Northwest, hops and barley needed to be imported, while crabapples were native and everywhere. Thus, cider was the beverage of choice over beer. It was even used as currency. It enjoyed its ubiquity until the temperance movement and, later, Prohibition stifled its popularity. However, its renaissance was on the horizon.

"Cider" apples ("spitters," to use the colloquial term) differ from "eating" apples in their increased bitterness and sour flavor. They are labeled as sweets, sharps, bittersharps, and bittersweets. When pressed into cider, they create tasting profiles that simply are not found in those Fujis and Honeycrisps we purchase by the pound in grocery stores. In Washington State, apple orchards were in all quarters, from horizon to horizon; however, the fruits required for tasty cider were harder to find. Enter Craig and Sharon Campbell.

"Everyone told me you can't grow cider apples in eastern Washington, in the Yakima Valley," recalls Craig. "I just thought, this is crazy, I can grow every other kind of fruit." With his wife, Sharon, the couple planted a small test orchard of cider apples alongside their other fruits on their 400-acre orchard east of the Cascades in 2008. Today, their commercial cidery, Tieton Cider Works, is fueled by their orchard, one of the largest in the country since they expanded their cider apple "experiment" from two acres to thirty. Greg and Sharon read the winds on the American booze market, which was just starting to see an uptick in demand for craft ciders in the early 2000s. Today, it's a full-on revolution, eclipsing even the craft beer industry.

HOW TO MAKE CIDER AT HOME

What you will need:
- Apples! (20 lbs. of apples creates 4.5 liters of juice.)
- Sanitizer spray
- Press or juicer (or you can pay to have your apples juiced)
- Knife and chopping board
- Bucket (food grade)
- Sieve
- Funnel
- Muslin or cheesecloth
- Clean towels
- Demijohn
- 1 campden tablet (optional)
- 1 packet yeast (optional)
- Bung and airlock
- Bottles and caps

This method uses traditional "wild fermentation," without the addition of campden tablets (for killing bacteria) or yeast. However, you are welcome to use both.

1 Sanitize all surfaces and equipment.
2 Wash, chop, and juice/press your apples.
3 Strain the juice through a cheesecloth into the demijohn.
4 Add 1 campden tablet and let the juice sit for 24 hours (optional).
5 Add 1 packet yeast (optional).
6 Fit bung and airlock into the demijohn.
7 Pour some cold water into your airlock. Then push the bung into the demijohn and push the airlock into the hole in the bung.
8 Put the cap on top of the airlock.
9 Let the juice ferment at room temperature for about 4 weeks. (The higher the sugar content of the apples, the longer fermentation will take.)
10 Bottle, cap, and enjoy! (For sparkling cider, add 1 tsp. granulated sugar before capping.)

HOPS

—

Hops are the flowers of the plant *Humulus lupulus* that, when dried, are the principal ingredient that gives beer a citrusy, bitter punch. A member of the Cannabaceae order (a relative to cannabis), hops were first cultivated in Europe. Initially, the eastern United States produced most U.S. hops. Post Prohibition, Washington State now grows the majority (77 percent).

- Most of the nation's hops are grown in Washington, Oregon, and Idaho. Washington produces over ¾ of that crop.

- Cascade, Mosaic, Centennial, and Citra are the most popular varieties.

- Hop acreage has doubled in the past decade.

- In 2021, La Niña and a heat wave (several days over 100°F) caused production to drop by nearly 10 percent.

- The climate, soils, water, and absence of pests in the Pacific Northwest allows for its dominance in hop production.

- An average acre of hops grows about 900 plants (or "hills").

- Each hill yields about 2 pounds of dried hop cones.

- 75 percent of all US hop acreage is in Yakima Valley.

- The Valley comprises three regions, each with different characteristics: the Moxee Valley, the Yakama Indian Reservation, and the Lower Yakima Valley.

Get to Know Your PNW Hops

- Cascade: Introduced in 1972, Cascade hops are the mainstay of the region. It has a relatively lower level of alpha acid—which means it imparts fewer bitter flavors into beer—and so it is mostly prized for its aroma. Cascade has notes of floral grapefruit.

- Centennial: Released in 1990, the high alpha content and pungent aroma make this hop bitter, with fantastic bouquet. (It has double the alphas of Cascade hops.)

- Citra: The third member of the "Three C's," released in 2007, this relative newcomer is popular for American ale-style brews. Citra has juicy citrus notes and is often used in tandem with Mosaic and Amarillo.

- Simcoe: This hop, introduced in 2000, has both distinctive bitterness and odor, making it a piney delight.

- Mosaic: Aptly named for its concert of flavors, this hop is all the rage in PNW pales and IPAs with its tropical fruit and pine notes.

- Chinook: With its super-high alpha content, this hop causes a lot of bitterness. Just like Prohibition.

- Amarillo: Grown exclusively in the Yakima Valley, Amarillo has the highest myrcene content of the region's hops, meaning its perfume is bolder than all the others. It imparts fruity, sweet notes to any brew.

JUNIPER

—

Beloved, we join hands here to pray for gin.
An aridity defiles us. Our innards thirst for the juice of juniper . . .
–Wallace Thurman, *Infants of the Spring*

Junipers thrive in Oregon. Scarcely found in Washington, Idaho, or British Columbia, there are large swaths of the Beaver State wherein the western juniper (the most abundant species) is the only tree that grows. They are conifers, but instead of cones they produce blue berries, coveted for their botanicals. It's no wonder that Oregon is producing some of the finest gins in the United States.

- The twistiness of the juniper's trunk makes it unsuitable for wood planks.

- The trees are so prolific in Oregon that they resemble an invasive species.

- Cedar Apple Rust, a fungus, is harmful to apples and found naturally on juniper trees. That's why you will not find both types of trees in the same orchard.

- Juniper berries are used in cooking venison to rid the meat of its gamey taste.

- Juniper berries are an excellent source of vitamin C and detoxifiers.

- The word gin comes from *genever*, the Dutch name for juniper.

- Female juniper trees produce the berries we consume; those from male trees are inedible.

- Juniper berries contain essential oils that act as anti-inflammatories.

- Consuming too many berries over a long period of time can cause kidney problems.

- Juniper berry oil has been shown to decrease anxiety when consumed.

GRAPES

—

"You are but a tiny cluster upon the vines of heaven, where the grapes are worlds;
yet you hold the power to ripen your bitter berries and add to the eternal vintage of
cosmic sweetness if so you will."
–Eden Phillpotts, *Saurus*

- Washington is the second-largest wine producer in the U.S., with over 1,000 wineries.

- Vineyards in Oregon use the equivalent of 35,000 football fields of land, and Washington vineyards use the equivalent of 60,000. Idaho is catching up with about 1,700.

- It takes three years after planting for vines to produce grapes.

- The amount of sugar in grapes is measured on the Brix scale.

- It takes one cluster of grapes to produce a glass of wine, and an entire grapevine to produce ten bottles of wine.

- Grapes are technically berries, not fruit.

- Grapes are the most prevalent fruit grown in the entire world.

- Wine grapes are grown on Antarctica.

Grow Your Own Grapes

Whether you want table grapes for snacking or you want to experiment with homemade wine, growing your own backyard grapes in the Pacific Northwest is easier than you think. Our climate and lack of pests create ideal growing conditions, and a few vines can produce dozens of pounds of grapes with relatively little space.

- Choose your location.

- You will need enough room for a strong trellis (enough to support up to 30 lbs. of fruit).

- Sun and airflow are key; your setup should face north/south to maximize both.

- Test your soil and adjust the pH balance as necessary—usually between 6.5 and 7.2 for most varieties. (This process can take some time, but your vines can last a century or more, so a little forethought can go a long way.)

- Purchase certified vines. (And, of course, shop local!)

- Prune, prune, prune!

Salmon-Safe

—

"OUR MISSION IS TO TRANSFORM land management practices so Pacific salmon can thrive in West Coast watersheds," is the straightforward declaration of Salmon-Safe, the organization that accredits farmers and producers as protectors of the emblematic staple fish so revered as food and as sport. Their network of place-based conservationists and collaborating certification organizations spans from California to Alaska, including the Columbia River Basin and Puget Sound, advocating for development practices, farming, and production methods that reduce impact on watersheds and salmon habitats. These practices include planting shade trees along waterways, using natural pesticides (i.e., helping bigger things eat the pests), and planting cover crops to mitigate topsoil erosion. They publish a running list of Salmon-Safe wine, beer, and food producers.

BEER

Deschutes Brewery

Ale Apothecary

Crux Fermentation
Project

Bevel Craft Brewing

Ninkasi Brewing

ColdFire Brewing

Ecliptic Brewing

Great Notion

CIDER

Fortune & Glory
Cider Company

Ten Towers Cider Co.

Reverend Nat's Hard
Cider

Legend Cider
Company

WINE

King Estate Winery

Abacela Winery

Melrose Vineyards

SPIRITS

Ewing Young
Distillery

Freeland Spirits

Hood River Distillers

Ransom Spirits

OREGON

ASTORIA

PORTLAND

NEWBERG   HOOD RIVER

SHERIDAN   SALEM

EUGENE   BEND

ROSEBURG   LA PINE

OREGON

———

PORTLAND, EUGENE, AND BEND are the vertices of a triangle, within which some fantastic booze is being produced. Oregon's Pinot Noirs solicit more awards every year; their beers are sold throughout the world; and their junipers impart the essence for truly exciting gins. Bend is quickly becoming as known for its suds as it is for its ski lodges.

OREGON
BEER

—

O regon's true original brewer was Henry Weinhard, who founded one of the territory's first beer-making establishments. In 1856, he lugged his 300-gallon copper brew kettle across the country to brew steam beer at Fort Vancouver Brewing (on the other side of the Columbia River from Portland). In 1928, his enterprise merged with Arnold Blitz's Oregon company to form Blitz-Weinhard Brewing in Portland. They were very successful in the midst of Prohibition until they ran into fierce competition with St. Louis, and they were eventually gobbled up by bigger companies.

Oregon's first contemporary brewery was launched in 1980 by Californian Charles Coury, who came from the wine business. It began as a misadventure, Coury's wine expertise failing him as a beermaker. "His initial goal was to make a 'mild ale,' a beer with a low taste profile, which could compete with Portland's Blitz-Weinhard," writes Fred Eckhardt. "His equipment was ancient and makeshift. The brew kettle was an old steam-jacketed dairy vessel as was the 'mash tun.' The mash tun had a makeshift wooden false-bottom strainer and, worse, the mash stood overnight before running off in the morning." The result was a wretched, smelly brew the locals scoffed at with its $1 price tag.

Serendipitously, a local home brewer named Tom Burns visited Coury seeking a job. Admitting defeat, Charles hired Tom and heeded his advice to implement bottle-conditioning (for higher ABV) and adding more hops to mask the unlikable flavor. Their new product was objectively better, but the locals—turned off by the initial products—were reluctant to try it. Unfortunately, a summer heat wave arrived at this very time, raising the brewery's ambient temperature so high that their entire batch turned sour. Coury and his wife Shirley gave up and left Oregon.

Learning from Coury's mistakes, Dick Ponzi, his wife, Nancy, and Karl Ockert opened BridgePort Brewing Company in 1984, focusing on English-style ales using local malts and hops. At that time, there were fewer than two dozen microbreweries in the entire country, a third of those being in Washington. Their mission was to launch a brewpub, wherein Portlanders could enjoy a pint at the very place it was brewed. However, Oregon law prohibited this—one could brew beer and sell wholesale, or sell beer retail at a bar, but not both. The following year in 1985, appreciating the potential of the market, the state passed a new law allowing for brewpubs. The Ponzis and Ockert pounced, opening the BridgePort BrewPub in 1986 where visitors could toss a few back while gazing upon their European-influenced cask-conditioning process.

The Widmer brothers, Kurt and Rob, soon entered the ring, serving their German-style ales just a block away from BridgePort. Soon, they were garnishing their Widmer hefeweizen brews with lemon slices and captivating the public, skyrocketing their brand to the most popular beer in the state. Within a few months, Fred Bowman and Art Larrance launched the state's third microbrewery, Portland Brewing, which was the first outlet in the state to feature Bert Grant's Scottish Ale (as well as their own popular Portland Ale). Oregon's nascent craft beer scene was off to the races.

Enter Brian and Mike McMenamin, whose bar and restaurant empire started with the Hillsdale Public House in 1985. The combination of the brothers' unique, interesting experimentals, paired with flavorful pub food, was a quick hit, and they were soon embraced by the public. They are especially known for their practice of taking over beloved, neglected buildings in the Pacific Northwest, renovating them, and re-launching the spaces as brewpubs; Edgefield, Kennedy School, and Portland's Bagdad Theater are just some successful examples.

The coming years would advance Oregon's dominance as a craft beer haven with the openings of Full Sail Brewing and Oregon Trail Brewery (1987), Deschutes and Rogue (1989), and the inaugural and hugely successful Oregon Brewers Festival (1988).

Deschutes Brewery

Bend, Oregon

 When Gary Fish founded Deschutes in 1988, he never dreamed that within a few decades his beers would be sold in 32 states and multiple countries. Eschewing the region's love of pale ales, he began it all with the iconic Black Butte Porter, which is now the top-selling porter in the United States. As *Craft Beer and Brewing* put it, "[Gary] thought it had all the elements that would appeal to customers just encountering craft beer for the first time." Deschutes now produces over 250,000 barrels per year of their Classics, Fresh Family Line, Seasonal, and Limited Release beers, as well as their non-alcoholic brews.

It all began with the Bend Public House, where they first brewed Black Butte in their ten-barrel brewhouse. The space has always served as a community gathering place for locals and tourists alike and is now a landmark in downtown

Bend. "I always knew that my friends would be there," explains Communications Manager Erin Rankin, "because Deschutes equals community." With 19 taps and a curated menu using locally sourced ingredients, this brewpub is a must-visit for the beer traveler. "We live where people come to vacation," says Brewmaster Scott Birdwell, "and beer and outdoors go together." Stop by for their "Hoppy Hour" food and drink specials, elk burger, blackened salmon BLT, or havarti mac and cheese. There is also the Bend Tasting Room and Beer Garden, a five-minute drive across the Deschutes River, where guests can fill up their growlers, take a brewery tour, and snag their favorite merch. Both spots are family-friendly and dog-friendly (on the patios).

A mainstay brand like Deschutes had to keep growing—so they launched their Portland Public House in the Rose City in 2008. Twenty-six taps serve up their classics, seasonals, and experimental brews. Executive Chef Jill Ramseier curates an incredible menu, caramelizing onions for their mac and cheese with Black Butte Porter, brining pickles for burgers with beer while smothering them with local Tillamook cheddar, and serving up a crab roll with local Pacific Northwest Dungeness crab. Smothered tots and pickle plates are available during happy hour, and they take care of their own with Service Industry Night specials on Mondays. At the end of your trip, you can even relive the experience at PDX at their Portland Airport Pub where you can relax with a pint and take some Fresh Squeezed IPA home with you.

Sustainability is essential to the Deschutes brand, and they walk the walk. They source a significant amount of their energy needs from wind and solar. They have also equipped a nighttime cooling system that prevents the need for air conditioning, insulated every possible inch of space to reduce energy use,

and installed a CO_2 vaporizer to abate their electricity demands. Recycling and composting are mainstay processes here, and ingredients for their beer and their food are as locally sourced as possible.

Products:

Fresh Family Line (year round)

- Fresh Squeezed IPA—citrusy hops and malt
- Fresh Haze IPA—cool and refreshing
- Hazetron Imperial Hazy IPA—tropical, hoppy flavor

Classics Line (year round)

- Black Butte Porter—where it all began; chocolate and coffee notes
- Mirror Pond Pale Ale—Cascade hops and caramel malt flavors
- King Crispy Pilsner—German-style "crisp pilsner"
- Obsidian Stout—black barley and espresso notes

Ale Apothecary

Bend, Oregon

 Founder Paul Arney grew up in an apothecary family. His great grandfather, C.B. Neihart, owned Neihart Drug in Coulee City, Washington, at the turn of the 20th century, selling alcohol prescriptions during Prohibition. C.B.'s son, Paul, took over the family business upon C.B.'s death, running the store with his wife, Pauline, and licensing it as the first state-run liquor store in Washington. Grandpa Paul's daughter, Patti, then married pharmacist Buzz Arney, who owned and operated the Silver Lake Pharmacy. When it came time for grandson Paul to open up his own business, he drew upon the family namesake for inspiration and founded Ale Apothecary brewery in 2012.

"I have made efforts to make my brewing process unique to our brewery," Paul explains, "because I feel that, along with ingredient selection and yeast, the brewing process adds 'house character' so the more interesting the process, the more interesting the beer. I have committed to acquiring local ingredients: our barley is grown and malted in Madras, our hops are grown in Silverton. I have also committed to utilizing the rawest and least-processed raw materials to brew within my efforts to remove the fingerprint of industrialization."

Paul's beers are unique, indeed. Every brew is barrel aged, and "bottle-conditioned"—meaning the carbonation is created by adding wildflower honey directly in the bottle, then yeast. Most of their products spend at least a year in-barrel, then another six months in the bottle for the yeast to consume the honey sugars. "No one else can imitate us," explains Brewmaster Connor Currie, a Bend native who started at Ale Apothecary in 2014. However, he adds that brewing in Bend means community. "There's no competition," he says. "We all help each other out."

Their devotion to using 100 percent Oregon-sourced ingredients and single-farm hops results in some incredible flavors - and it all started with their Sahalie brew, a dry-hopped golden ale which Paul initially envisioned as the only beer they would sell. That quickly expanded to their menu of La Tache, barley-and-wheat malt flavored with Cascade hops; Ralph, a piney concoction brewed with fir needles; and El Cuatro, a dark ale started in pinot noir barrels and finished in brandy barrels. Their taproom also carries rotating "guest ciders" from other Bend producers. There is one thing you won't find there, however. "We don't do IPAs," Connor says proudly with a smile. Dogs are welcomed on the patio, and they are currently working with a local chef on a food pairing menu.

Crux Fermentation Project

Bend, Oregon

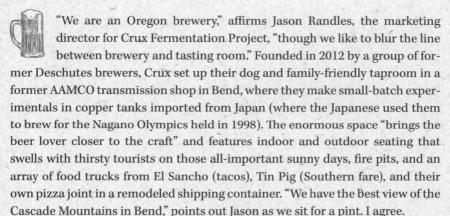 "We are an Oregon brewery," affirms Jason Randles, the marketing director for Crux Fermentation Project, "though we like to blur the line between brewery and tasting room." Founded in 2012 by a group of former Deschutes brewers, Crux set up their dog and family-friendly taproom in a former AAMCO transmission shop in Bend, where they make small-batch experimentals in copper tanks imported from Japan (where the Japanese used them to brew for the Nagano Olympics held in 1998). The enormous space "brings the beer lover closer to the craft" and features indoor and outdoor seating that swells with thirsty tourists on those all-important sunny days, fire pits, and an array of food trucks from El Sancho (tacos), Tin Pig (Southern fare), and their own pizza joint in a remodeled shipping container. "We have the best view of the Cascade Mountains in Bend," points out Jason as we sit for a pint. I agree.

The Crux team chose Bend for their project for the weather, community, water, and the proximity to local ingredients like hops and malt. They are committed to supporting local farmers and purchasing salmon-safe certified hops. "We try to do what's right," Jason explains. They contribute to charities such as the local Humane Society with regular "Pint Nights," as well as give to the Bend Sustainability Fund with fundraisers. At their mass-production facility, Brewmaster Cam O'Connor implements water-saving practices as he brews over 16,000 barrels per year for sale in five states. They also collaborate with Oregon State University (founder Larry Sidor's alma mater) for the school's fermentation science program.

Their Crux Pilz is their flagship product, a "beer for brewers" Jason explains. The taproom is the only place to taste the small-batch experimentals they brew in the Japanese copper kettles, so asking the bartender for recommendations is essential. We sampled their excellent Pre-Prohibition Lager and Glow Stick Hazy IPA as Jason explained their tasting notes with pride. In addition to tasty brews like their fruity sours and Half Hitch Imperial IPA with Mosaic hops, Crux always carries their NØ MØ and NØ MØ Hazy non-alcoholic IPAs for those who wish to slow down and the sober-curious. Barrel-aging is very much a part of the Crux Fermentation Project as well, using wine and bourbon barrels for some brews like their Tough Love Imperial Stout and offering two whiskies, a straight bourbon and another finished in stout barrels. Taproom visitors can fill their growlers and purchase make-your-own 4-packs of their canned perennial favorites, as well as taste rotating local wines and ciders from their Bend colleagues. Soon they plan to launch an in-house cocktail program here, as well as a sister pub in Portland.

Products:

- Crux Pilz—brewed with traditional pilsner malts and imported Czech Saaz and local Oregon Sterling hops; biscuity flavors, spicy herbal notes, and a hint of lemon

- NØ MØ—refreshingly hoppy with a familiar mouthfeel; a non-alcoholic IPA crafted with Citra and Mosaic hops

- PCT Porter—highly drinkable porter with rich, roasted aromas and notes of dark chocolate, with lasting smoothness and a sweet finish

- Doublecross—a single batch, annual winter release with vibrant reddish-black hue, substantial body, and pleasant headiness; intense flavors of dark candi sugar reminiscent of preserved fruits and holiday spicing

Bevel Craft Brewing

Bend, Oregon

 Bevel was born of disc golf. Founders Valarie and Nate Doss have seven national championships between them, and they met on the professional circuit. It all started with Valarie's family: her father was a homebrew enthusiast and as they toured the country for tournaments, her parents would always make it a point to stop at local breweries and sample their IPAs. When Nate (a "California boy," Valarie jokes) joined the family, their infectious worship of hops rubbed off on him and he began interning at Good Life Brewing in Bend, a city they chose for its affordability and tight-knit brewing community. As their respective disc golf careers wound down, they decided to combine their loves of sport and beer and launch Bevel in 2018. "We are here because we love beer," Valarie beams with pride.

Everything they do is hop-centric. Using Yakima Valley hops and locally sourced grain and malts, they carry several year-round core brews—including their flagship First Run IPA—in addition to many experimentals and seasonals, all of which are only available at their Bend taproom. "We don't overcomplicate things—we make beer for conversation," Valarie explains. She says that everything comes down to time and temperature as she shows me around the seven-barrel brewing space (the barrels named for important people in their lives).

The taproom is dog- and family-friendly, with a huge patio space in the back featuring four permanent food trucks serving street fare, tacos, and international dishes. Head Bartender Matt Dyer

poured me a tasting flight—an absolute must-try for visitors, as they serve the samples in customized Frisbees. Every day features different activities, like disc golf putting on Wednesdays, charity bingo on Mondays, and trivia nights. They contribute to the Bend chapter of the Pink Boots Society, which supports women brewers and local producers. Disc golf is always played on the televisions, and be prepared to learn the lingo as every brew is named in the sport's honor. The city's newest beer maker is already winning accolades, named by *Source Weekly* magazine as Central Oregon's "Best Brewer."

Products:

- Funday IPA—light, approachable with a low ABV

- Par Save Pale—bitter and crisp

- Scope of Resin IPA—tropical and hoppy

- Black Ace—award-winning Cascadian Dark Ale with bitter chocolate notes

- Hop Tour Series—rotating single-hopped experimentals

- Seasonal sours, lagers, and cold IPAs

Ninkasi Brewing

Eugene, Oregon

 Ninkasi was the Sumerian goddess of fermentation, so it's no wonder why founders Jamie Floyd and Nikos Ridge named their brewery in her honor. Jamie left California in 1990 to attend the University of Oregon, where he made his first homebrew. He applied his talents to working at Steelhead Brewery in Eugene for 11 years, taking what he learned to create his own endeavor in 2006 with Ninkasi's first batch of their now-iconic Total Domination Northwest IPA. Jamie and Nikos spent their first six months of the project brewing at a German restaurant, constantly expanding the company into what is now the 33rd-largest craft brewery in the United States, employing over 100 people.

As you walk past the sculpted-metal Tricerahops and enter Ninkasi's Better Living Room three-story atrium in Eugene, you will find much more than beer. The space is envisioned as a gathering place for beer, food, art, and community and features an outdoor patio for those sacred sunny PNW summer days and a rock-climbing wall (not open to guests to limit tomfoolery). Their small-batch limited release "pilot" brews can only be found here, along with their Core Brews and Legends of Ninkasi Comic Book Series of beers. They also have a unique canned cocktail program designed by Jeffrey Morgenthaler, featuring their Bourbon Renewal (bourbon, black currant, and lemon), Agave Paloma (grapefruit and jalapeño), Gin Rickey, Rum Punch with pineapple and almond, and Ginger Honey Press.

I was greeted with genuine smiles and incredible hospitality on my visit. The bartender, Brandy, served me up a flight (five, 5 oz. pours) of signature brews contrasted from light to dark, including informative cards for each that have tasting notes and ingredients. Hospitality Director Bryan Nelson stopped by to say hello and make sure that my fried rockfish sandwich was up to snuff (it was absolutely delicious, even to a Florida boy like myself who grew up on fish sammies). Marketing Manager Rebecca Pirwitz sat down with me for a pint to talk shop about working at Ninkasi. "I don't want to leave at 5 p.m. every day," she says laughingly.

"I love my job." Jamie stopped over to introduce himself—his positive energy contagious—as did Dr. Daniel Sharp, their brewmaster. It was readily apparent that the Better Living Room has a devoted fan base—truly a place where everybody knows your name, *Cheers*-style. The space has several bars available for private parties and weddings, and is family-friendly and welcoming to doggos.

Products:

- Whit Rapids—named after their Eugene neighborhood with coriander and orange notes
- Total Domination Northwest IPA—their first and flagship hoppy masterpiece with piney grapefruit
- Tricerahops Double IPA—floral, citrusy hop jubilee
- Prismatic Juicy IPA—six types of hops flavor this tropical hit
- Trailhead Tropical IPA— tastes of mango and papaya
- Dawn of the Red IPA—malty pineapple delight
- Oatis Oatmeal Stout—rich, chocolatey, and delicious

Legends of Ninkasi Series

- Eclipsosaurus Hazy IPA; Velocihoptor Juicy IPA; Megaladom Triple IPA

Canned Cocktails by Jeffrey Morgenthaler

- Bourbon Renewal; Agave Paloma; Gin Rickey; Rum Punch; Ginger Honey Press; Grapefruit Refresher

ColdFire Brewing

Eugene, Oregon

 ColdFire Brewing is proof that it's never too late to change trajectory and follow your passion. Brothers Dan and Stephen Hughes were successful professionals—Stephen a microbiologist and Dan a healthcare manager—who quit their lucrative jobs to make beer full time at their reclaimed brewery and taproom in Eugene, Oregon. "It's not about the money," says Dan. They grew up homebrewing, and when they both found themselves burning out in their respective careers they walked away from job security and salaries to start interning at local breweries, learning the craft and applying their extensive knowledge of microbiology to their own concoctions, with their focus on flavor. "You can make a flawless beer that is totally undrinkable," they explain. Their

friendly and engaging bartender poured me a flight of her favorite brews, and after my first sip I was grateful that the brothers had chased their dream.

They launched their public house in 2016, starting with three fermenters making European-inspired small-batch brews. Cumulus Tropicalus is the flagship beer, a must-try full-bodied hoppy delight; Thursday/Friday IPA is full of citrus and hops; and they feature fantastic sours, Czech and German–style pilsners, dunkel lager, and barrel-aged experimentals. Their Valley Mèlange recently won a World Cup Beer Award in 2022. Dan and Stephen are family men, so the space is family-friendly (the first brewery in Eugene with a changing table!) and dog-friendly. Food trucks are always on site, with a rotating schedule of offerings featuring noodles, barbeque, and pizza.

Products:

- Capulus Robustus Stout—Brazilian and Sumatran coffees with Madagascar vanilla

- Spring IPA—tangerine, orange blossom, and Jolly Rancher notes

- Skyline Dreams—gooseberries, ripe mango, orange, and lemon zests

- Czech Pilsner—well-rounded lager with spice and honey notes

- ColdFire Pilsner—German-style with just the right amount of bitterness

- Munich Dunkel Lager—rich, bready, sweet flavors

Ecliptic Brewing

Portland, Oregon

 John Harris is an award-winning veteran of the brewing industry in Oregon. After launching Deschutes as the brewmaster in 1988, he joined the team at Full Sail Brewing in the early 1990s. In 2013 he put his own enterprise in motion, founding Ecliptic Brewing in Portland. The name is born of his two passions, beers and astronomy; just as the Earth revolves around the sun, Ecliptic creates seasonal brews for every time of year.

They have two locations: "The Mothership" in North Portland—where they brew and operate a full-service restaurant—and The Moon Room in the Southeast, which is a taproom only. At the restaurant, visitors can find burger-and-beer specials, trivia nights, and a menu featuring local, seasonal ingredients on dishes like their Beet Melt sandwich and Curried Cauliflower Fritters. Dogs are welcome on the patio, and the family-friendly space features a kids menu as well. Growler fills and kegs are available—but stay for a pint or two.

Products:

- Starburst IPA—A starburst galaxy produces an exceptionally high amount of stars, similar to how Ecliptic Starburst IPA produces a soaring amount of hop flavor. Brewed with Amarillo, Azacca, Centennial, Citra, Mosaic, and Simcoe hops for fresh flavors of citrus, fruit, and pine. 100 percent Pale malt makes for a super clean finish and puts the focus on the hop flavors and aromas. Dry-hopped to the end of the universe

- Carina—Carina Peach Sour Ale takes its name from the constellation Carina, the keel of the ship Argo in the southern sky. Loaded with fresh peach flavor, Carina is a sour ale perfect for any time of year

- Tucana—Named after a constellation of stars, Tucana Tangerine Sour Ale is crisp and refreshing, with a touch of tangerine that plays nicely with its well-balanced tartness

- Capella—Capella Porter is named after a bright star in the constellation Auriga. Sweet dark malt aromas are followed by a nice medium body. Flavors of chocolate and caramel meld with just a touch of roast

Great Notion

Portland, Oregon, and Seattle, Washington

 Paul Reiter, James Dugan, and Andy Miller all lived on the same block - they were neighbors and friends. One night, Paul was walking home with his family after dinner and shared some beers with James and Andy from their homebrewing project. "I'm pretty sure they let me try their homebrew hazy IPA," Paul recalls, "and it blew my mind. I asked them if they planned on selling this stuff, but neither of them wanted to talk to bankers, lawyers, or accountants—so we just kind of formed like Voltron between an artist, a scientist, and a businessperson." From this collaboration formed Great Notion brewing.

They have an eye for sustainable production methods, sourcing local produce for their kettle sours and barrel-aged sours. They also conserve water by recycling it from the whirlpool to their hot liquor tank during the brewing process. Additionally, all spent grain goes to local farmers.

Taprooms:

Oregon

- Alberta (Portland, OR):
  Dog-friendly, kid-friendly, great beer garden and space indoors. Food provided by the amazing award-winning Matt's BBQ Tacos

- Beaverton
  Kid-friendly, dog-friendly, great food provided by Great Notion

- NW 28th Ave (Portland)
Kid friendly, awesome kitchen with food provided by Great Notion, beautiful taproom with views into their production facility

- Division Pop-Up:
A fun outdoor space during warm months. Kid and dog friendly. Food provided by food trucks

Seattle, Washington:
- Ballard
A gorgeous new space that is family and dog friendly, featuring a menu from Burb's Burgers

- Georgetown
Taproom with a patio. Guests may bring in their own food

Products:

- Ripe IPA—A super-crushable all-Citra hazy IPA with tropical notes of mango and papaya

- Over Ripe Hazy IPA—dry-hopped with plenty of mango-heavy Azacca hops, while the Citra and Motueka hops add every color of citrus fruit to the aroma

- Blueberry Muffin Fruited Sour Ale—tastes just like a blueberry muffin made with Oregon blueberries and baked to perfection

- Double Stack Imperial Breakfast Stout—robust dark chocolate and caramel flavors imparted by Mostra Coffee's Ghost Bear beans, creating a rich, chewy mouthfeel and sweet flavor of maple syrup

OREGON
CIDER

—

Fortune & Glory Cider

Astoria, Oregon

 "Original" is a fitting word for Fortune & Glory. Founded by Jeremy Towsey-French in 2017, they are Astoria's original cider producer:

What started as one person's awakening grew considerably, joining a long line of enterprises that define the story of Astoria: a city forged by the will and desires of enterprising people for more than 200 years. . . a place where those who envision things bigger than themselves can find their fortune and their glory, whatever that may be.

Their ciders are original as well—like, really original. Though they use Northwest fruits, their recipes are sourced from pre-Prohibition farmhouse (Belgian) and pub-style (English) techniques:

Once established in the New World, early American settlers took to making the hearty hard ciders so common in their homeland. The simple and tasty byproduct of farmhouse ale production (as they leveraged the leftover yeast from beer fermentation), these utility ciders quickly found appeal among a wide array of drinkers spanning the social strata. Utility ciders thus formed the foundation of America's original hard cider recipes, where protecting the sanctity of individual apple varieties was secondary to generating yeasty, bold, and deeply satisfying farmhouse cider profiles.

Fortune & Glory is committed to reproducing the unique taste and character of the old-world European utility ciders that powered our early American ancestors so long ago –and do again today.

Their Astoria taproom—a renovated auto repair shop—has something for everyone. Dogs and vegans are welcome. They always have a local beer on tap for the apple-weary, and zero-proof cocktails and NA brews for the teetotalers. Homemade Liege waffles are baked fresh every day, and their signature cheese dish, "The Ball," features toasted pecans and seasoned peppers, served with Ritz crackers (in-line with their "original" ethos, it comes from an old family recipe). Consider a stop for dessert as well—their Budino is a cross between chocolate mousse and pudding, served with cranberry almond biscotti.

Every batch of Fortune & Glory hard cider is based on a different blend of northwest apples (typically eight to 12 varieties), which impart their own special character on every recipe. As such, while the cider names and recipes may stay the same, each batch is its own unique iteration, featuring incremental recipe changes to highlight and compliment the most dominant apple varieties in each batch. With Fortune & Glory hard cider, you can expect new layers of intrigue in every glass, as familiar styles unfold to expose new flavors and experiences.

Products:

- Strawberry Feels—a crisp, English-style apple pub cider, with Northwest strawberries and fresh lemon zest, and including pomegranate and raspberry leaves, hibiscus, rose hips, and chicory

- Black Lodge—their popular marionberry pub cider fermented with English ale yeast for a crisp, country pub finish, reminiscent of a clean London metro ale; lightly infused with botanicals, including hibiscus, rosehips, chicory, orange peel, and blackberry leaves

- Razzberet—a semi-dry fruited farmhouse cider slowly fermented using Belgian saison yeast; paired with Willamette Valley raspberries, blackberry leaves, rose hips, and hibiscus to bring about a tart and sharp profile that finishes smooth and easy

- Blood Moon—a big-bodied Belgian farmhouse cider with a light kiss of blood orange zest gently accentuating a tart blend of table apples; smooth, dry, and oaky, with the subtle addition of rose hips, hibiscus, blackberry leaves, orange peel, and hawthorn

Ten Towers Cider Co.

Salem, Oregon

Since 1972, the Kruger family has been making cider from the neighborhood orchards. We grew well known varieties like Red Delicious, Crispin, Liberty, Freedom, King, Fuji, and more. I started Ten Towers Cider Co. in 2017 with a mission to create high quality Pacific Northwest craft ciders. Through teamwork, innovation, and creativity, we deliver our customers the best experience, one bottle at a time.

Products:

- Shakti—delicately spiced with chai tea
- Gravitas—a perfect coalescence of cold-pressed Pacific Northwest apples and unyielding spirit years in the making
- Soulless Pear—Northwest pear and apple give breath to Soulless Pear's haunting ginger essence
- Unmatched—fresh-pressed Pacific Northwest pink lady apples with a slightly tart and semi-sweet balance

Reverend Nat's Hard Cider

Portland, Oregon

Reverend Nat is a single-minded cider evangelist and craft beer revolutionary who searches the world for superior ingredients to handcraft the most unusual ciders that no one else will make.

Nat West's neighbor had a big apple tree. For years they sourced its fruit to make pies, apple sauce, apple butter, and snacks. One day, a light bulb flashed: why not make *cider*? He fashioned a makeshift juice press in his garage from a jack and some timber, and after tasting the results of his hard labor, he was hooked. He made 5 gallons of cider, then 15, then 40. Within a few years, he had amassed 500 gallons in his basement, from which neighbors would fill up mason jars of the fruity stock when they stopped by. He experimented with yeasts, spices, hops, and fruit juices, embracing forgotten methods and old-world techniques from his impressive library of cider-making books in an effort to produce one-of-a-kind brews that could be found nowhere else.

By 2023, Reverend Nat's had set up shop in Portland, serving their flagship products and one-off experimentals at their taproom and brewery. Visitors enjoy local guest beers, kombucha, and food from Farmhouse Food Carts next door. Flights, exclusive batches, pints, and growlers are all available (bring the kids, but leave the puppies at home).

"It began with Revival, my deeply complex yet subtly familiar apple cider, and the radical Hallelujah Hopricot, a 'beer, cider and wine all in one,'" explains Nat. "Now I make four year-round ciders including my multiple award-winning Sacrilege Sour Cherry and the truly compelling Deliverance Ginger Tonic."

Products:

- Revival Hard Apple—a secret blend of Washington-grown apples and piloncillo (dark brown evaporated cane juice) purchased direct from Michoacán, Mexico; brilliantly golden in color and deeply complex while remaining subtly familiar, with just the right amount of sweetness and acidity to be an everyday beverage

- Sacrilege Sour Cherry—100 percent sour Granny Smith apples unified with the superior Montmorency sour cherry and the exotic Morello sour cherry (hailing from my native country of Hungary), rounded out with a spot of Bartlett pear juice and completed with a touch of spiciness (largely attributable to the ghost chili pepper, although married with a secret spice)

- Viva La Pineapple—a blend of fermented fresh apple juice and unfermented fresh pineapple juice, with a touch of spice (cinnamon, cloves, and allspice)

Legend Cider Company

La Pine, Oregon

Legend Cider Company founders Adrianne and Tyler Baumann had a mission: to launch a craft cider company in a small Oregon town that produced natural cider without added sugar. "Cider had a bad reputation," Adrianne explains at their boutique taproom in La Pine, a 30-minute drive south of Bend. "We did not enjoy all the sweet, dry ciders that were around." The self-taught couple started making cider via trial and error in 2015 in The Dalles, but decided to relocate to La Pine and launch their tasting room in 2019. "We are focused on helping small towns grow," Adrianne explains with pride. "We found support here in La Pine. We've always loved drinking cider—now we get to love making it."

The Baumanns only use fresh apple juice and yeast in their production - no added sugars or water. The cold-control process allows the yeast to work its magic without the need to kill it with chemicals. Their unfiltered recipes are sourced from the American Colonial period, when cider was ubiquitous, and their apples are gathered from Hood River, with additional fruits sourced as locally as possible. Adrianne poured me a pint of their flagship Pacific POG (pineapple, orange, guava) before showing me around their taproom; the drink has a beautiful color, and is infinitely drinkable without the sugar rush of "fake" national brands. "Flavor profile is the most important," she says.

Their family-friendly La Pine taproom has a fantastic selection of ciders, of which visitors can grab a pint or fill a growler. For locals, the Mug Club ($95/year) gets them unlimited 20 oz. pours at pint prices. They partnered with local food truck El Buen Zason del Mago to offer tacos and tamales every day, so you have every excuse to post up at their bar (engraved with a representation of the Cascade Mountains) and chat with the locals—even those who normally drink beer. "There's a masculine hesitancy about trying cider," Adrianne claims, and I agree—but who doesn't like to catch a buzz while drinking apple juice? They have bingo on Wednesdays, with proceeds donated to local charities, and guests are welcome to play "cider pong" in the back room.

Products:

- PCT Punch—juicy and tropical with pineapple and coconut juices

- Siskiyou Strawberry Lemonade—a blend of real strawberry and lemonade juices

- Columbia Gorge Grape— like a juicebox from childhood, only more fun

- Pioneer Punch—mango, pineapple, kiwi, and lime

- Paulina Pomegranate—pomegranate and cranberry juices

OREGON
WINE

—

Oregonians were growing and fermenting grapes before we achieved statehood.
But our current reputation as one of the world's top producers of high-quality wine
has been built over the past five decades.
–Oregon Wine Board

In 1847, pioneer Henderson Luelling and his family arrived in the Oregon Territory from Iowa. They brought with them several dozen varieties of fruit up the Oregon Trail, including Oregon's first grapes. Five years later, Peter Britt, a Swiss immigrant, established the Northwest's first winery, Valley View, in Jacksonville. Britt is now venerated as "The Father of the Southern Oregon fruit industry." After Statehood in 1859, Adam Doerner, a German winemaker, planted grapes on his farm in the Umpqua Valley. He grew Zinfandel, Riesling, and a Sauvignon varietal, making wine and brandy. The vineyard bears fruit to this day. By 1904, Oregon was winning its first winemaking awards for Riesling at the World's Fair.

Like their neighbors to the north in Washington, zealous Oregon voters passed Prohibition in 1916, three years before it went nationwide. John Wood and Ron Honeyman of Salem were among a group of early Oregon entrepreneurs who received bonded winery status shortly after Prohibition's repeal. Honeywood Winery is Oregon's oldest continuously operating winery and holds bonded winery number 26.

Richard Sommer ushered in Oregon's modern winemaking era in 1962, planting Riesling, Gewürztraminer, chardonnay, sémillon, sauvignon blanc, cabernet sauvignon, pinot noir, Malbec, and zinfandel at his HillCrest Vineyard in the Umpqua Valley. HillCrest, which holds bonded winery certificate number 42, is Oregon's oldest estate winery. It was at this time (1964) that food raconteur (and Portland native) James Beard published his memoir *Delights and Prejudices*, gaining the Beaver State national culinary notoriety.

In February 1965, David Lett first rooted pinot noir cuttings near Corvallis - the first plantings in the Willamette Valley. Chuck and Shirley Coury arrived in March and planted their first vines in the nursery established by Lett, leaving them to his care. The couple had been warned that "the rain would wash them out, they would grow fungus between their toes, it would rot their clothes off, and there was no way in hell they would be able to grow great grapes up here." They returned later on and purchased land in Forest Grove, on a site that had operated a vineyard and winery from the mid-1800s through Prohibition, seeding it with pinot noir and riesling. This vineyard is now called David Hill.

Tualatin Estate Vineyard, established in 1973 by Bill Fuller and Bill Malkmus, is one of the most venerated vineyards in Oregon. Both its red and white varietals were awarded Best in Show at the London International Wine Competition, and it is the only Oregon winery to win the Governor's Award (the state's most illustrious) in sequential years. In 1975, Cal Knudsen and Dick Erath launched Knudsen-Erath Winery as Bonded Winery No. 52, the first commercial winery in the Dundee Hills.

The 1980s witnessed ups, downs, landmark innovation, and disappointment. In 1983, the Willamette Valley American Viticulture Area (AVA) was established as Oregon's first such designation. In 1984, Umpqua Valley vintner Scott Henry designed a unique four-pronged trellising system that exposes grape clusters to maximum sunlight. The Scott Henry Trellis System was rapidly adopted by vineyards all over the world. This same year was known as the state's worst harvest season, a victim of extreme precipitation, frosty weather, and late ripening. The season did end on a high note, as the Oregon Wine Board began funding an enology program at Oregon State University (OSU). At the close of the decade, phylloxera—the vine-root louse—arose in Willamette Valley, "forcing vineyard owners," according to the Oregon Wine Board, "to rip out vines and replant on grafted phylloxera-resistant rootstock; the process is expensive, labor-intensive, and heartbreaking."

In the 2000s, Oregon winemaking experienced several sea changes. First, Carlton Winemakers Studio appeared as the first multiple-winery facility in the state. Then, A to Z Wineworks debuted the Négociant Model, wherein finished wine is bought in bulk, blended, and resold on a new label. The model clicked with the public, and A to Z quickly grew to be Oregon's largest winery.

Laurent Montalieu, owner of the NW Wine Company in McMinnville, and his partners created the "custom crush" model that sources, farms, crushes, and vinifies fruit for the customer before it's bottled with custom labeling. During this decade, the Columbia Gorge, Southern Oregon, Dundee Hills, Yamhill-Carlton, McMinnville, Ribbon Ridge, Red Hill Douglas County, Chehalem Mountains, and Eola-Amity Hills AVAs were established. In 2008, Bertony Faustin founded Abbey Creek Vineyard in Portland, Oregon's first Black-owned-and-operated winery.

Today, there are 19 unique wine-growing regions in Oregon.

King Estate Winery

Eugene, Oregon

Founded in 1991 by Ed King Sr. and his son Ed King Jr., the eponymous King Estate Winery is North America's largest biodynamic vineyard, certified as organic before it was cool (2002), and they are obsessed with land stewardship as a guiding principle in their production. You will not find any herbicides, pesticides, or synthetic fertilizers on their sprawling acreage, as they approach their land use holistically, employing processes like crop rotation and composting in an effort to be sustainable and natural. Their products are certified Salmon-Safe as they also maintain 40 acres of endangered native oak woodlands on their property, filled with protected species. Their production is solar powered by an array of over 4,000 solar panels, and on the right day you can even witness them releasing rehabilitated owls and kestrels on their raptor release site in partnership with the local Cascades Raptor Center.

When sampling their wines, you may forget about all of the Kings' hard work on sustainable practices as the taste of the final product crisps your tongue. King Estate joined the Willamette Valley AVA in 2006, and their grapes are grown in Bellpine and Jory soils. The incredible drainage and moisture retention of this special land allows King Estate to forgo irrigation altogether, leading to more concentrated flavors in their fruit. The Estate has expanded significantly as the Kings purchased adjoining parcels, now totaling over 1,000 acres. Along with their family of vineyard partners, they grow almost every grape imaginable here: cabernet franc, tempranillo, syrah, and pinot noir; chardonnay, muscat, and riesling; sparkling blanc de gris, blanc de noirs, and brut cuvee; and rose of pinot noir. The winery is most known for its pinot gris. "King Estate is credited with creating the national market for Oregon pinot gris," explains Jenny Ulum, director of marketing. "Increasingly, we're developing a reputation for sauvignon blanc as well."

Visitors have every reason to stay and dine on-site at the King Estate Restaurant (open on weekends, reservations required). They offer a true farm-to-table experience for brunch, lunch, and dinner. Charcuterie, frittatas, and scallops are featured for brunch; swordfish, lamb, and octopus for lunch; and dinner guests can enjoy beef tenderloin, smoked chicken, and pot pies with vegetables grown on the estate.

Products:

- 2021 King Estate Pinot Gris—a must-try with aromas of peach, honeysuckle, and lime

- 2021 Sauvignon Blanc—pale lemon color with big, fruity nose

- 2016 Willamette Valley Chardonnay—French oak, vanilla, and wild honey

- 2012 North by Northwest Riesling—bright acidity; apricot and lemon custard

- 2017 Gewürztraminer— honeydew, apple, and mango

- 2016 Weinbau Cabernet Franc —plum, cassis, and pepper

- 2021 Inscription Pinot Noir—deep ruby color with raspberry and black plum

- 2016 Carpenter Hill Petite Sirah—inky purple color with currant, peppercorn, and espresso

- 2016 Tempranillo—brick-red with summer fruit flavors

- 2021 Rose of Pinot Noir—rose petals, bing cherry, and strawberry

Abacela Winery

Roseburg, Oregon

Abacela founder Earl Jones and his son, Greg, are obsessed with tempranillo, and we are all the better for it. After spending years researching the climate and geography of the Rioja and Ribera del Duero growing regions in Spain, Earl chose the Umpqua Valley in Oregon to establish his vineyard and bring the tempranillo grape successfully to the United States. The short growing season here is bookended by cool spring and autumn temperatures, which he discovered was the key to replicating the grape's fruition in Europe. The valley has a low risk of freezes, its climate created by the confluence of the Klamath Mountains, Oregon Coast Range, and the Cascade Range.

The estate comprises three main parcels: Cox's Rock, Cobblestone Hill, and Chaotic Ridge. There exist five types of soils across the vineyards: Sutherlin Silt Loam, Philomath-Dixonville Complex, Dickerson Loam, Nonpareil Loam, and Coburg Silt Loam, all of which require different irrigation and management

techniques. The entire acreage is biodynamic, maintained without the use of insecticides.

Jones is devoted to other sustainable practices in addition to the biodynamic ethos. In partnership with their neighbor Wildlife Safari, Abacela grows hay on their land and exchanges it with the animal refuge for elephant dung, perfect for fertilizing their grapes organically. Their tasting room is powered by geothermal energy, and they have set aside an astounding 300 acres for conservation.

Jones puts taste and quality above all else, as evidenced by Abacela's winemaking process. They only pick ripe fruit that they deem acceptable for their expressive wines, they utilize old oak barrels instead of new oak when possible to avoid overwhelming the flavors, and they only filter when necessary in an effort to leave all the grapes' characteristics in the final product. They implement whole berry fermentation using a gravity flow system—eschewing crushed must pulp in favor of inputting whole or partially crushed berries—which allows for an anaerobic fermentation that creates and maintains the grapes' beautiful aromatics.

At Abacela's tasting room, visitors can enjoy seated tastings both indoors or on their patio (reservations recommended). Small plates of hummus and cheeses are available. Their TGIF wine-and-pizza dinners on Fridays are very popular. Check their calendar for special events (like Valentine's Day dinners). Dogs are welcome outdoors.

Notable Wines from Abacela:

- Grenache—dark cherry, raspberry, plum, and lavender aromas

- Syrah—intense aromas, flavors, and tannic structure

- Malbec—aromas of blackberries, chocolate, oak, and dried lavender meld with broad tannins and an earthy spice

- Tannat—21 months in French oak; loaded with dark fruits, cracked pepper, and sweet tobacco

Melrose Vineyards

Roseburg, Oregon

Located on the South Umpqua River at the site of an early French settlement, Melrose Vineyards has been growing quality sauv blanc, chardonnay, tempranillo, malbec, and other grapes since 1996 on their 150 acres. Founder Wayne Parker arrived here with two decades of experience growing grapes for raisin production in the San Joaquin Valley; he appreciated great promise in the Southern Oregon terroir. Within months of planting, a 100-year flood besieged the vineyard, washing away five acres. Wayne persisted, however, and their delayed first crop yielded rave reviews. By 2000, they were producing their own wines, renovating a century-old bar into a welcoming tasting room with an outdoor balcony, panoramic views, and pet-friendly picnic and RV accommodations.

Products:

- 2020 Pinotage—an unmistakable soft velvet body with red fruit tones of pomegranate and raspberry and accompanying floral notes

- 2021 Baco Noir—aromas of candied bacon, black fruits, and ripe plum; smooth with low tannins, medium to high acidity with long lasting soft finish

- 2020 Malbec—deep purple appearance with black currant, dark plum, caramel, sweet tobacco, and smokiness aroma; hints of dark red cherry, plum, raspberry, toffee, red beet, and cranberry

- 2018 Dolcetto—cherry, leather, lilac, and coriander aromas, followed by the taste of black cherry, plum, cranberry, and cocoa butter

- 2015 Merlot—aromas of ivy, plum, cedar, truffle, and cream with tastes of pear, pie crust, cranberry, and a hint of mango

- 2015 Syrah—brick hues in color, with aromas of cigar box, cedar, plum, and lavender; tastes of allspice, lavender, and vanilla with hints of cinnamon

OREGON
SPIRITS
—

Ewing Young Distillery
Newberg, Oregon

 As we like to say at Ewing Young Distillery, Ewing Young helped take The Oregon Country from Great Britain without firing a shot—he did it by pouring a shot.™

The story of this distillery begins with Ewing Young. In fact, the *entire history of Oregon* begins with him. Nicknamed "The Captain," Young was a fur trader who arrived in the Oregon Territory in 1834, staking his claim in the Chehalem Valley (where the distillery is located today) as the westernmost farm in the United States, setting up a grist mill, saw mill, trading post, and bank. He began distilling "white lightning" moonshine spirits, to the consternation of the local British outpost and the Methodists. They refused to sell him cattle, but instead offered him money to quit distilling and leave the territory. He accepted the money, only to return soon after with 600 heads of longhorn cattle that he had driven from Mexico (the first documented cattle drive in North America). He died relatively young (no one knows his age for certain), as the richest man in Oregon. His grave is marked by an oak tree that

is now almost two centuries old, the landmark of what is now Ewing Young Distillery, created in his honor.

They label their distillations as Metaphysics in a Bottle, as they source spirits from producers along Young's traveled trails and then age, blend, and bottle them as their own. They also distill their own spirits. Visitors can sample flights and cocktails of their whiskies, vodkas, and gins at the tasting room on weekends, or purchase bottles on weekdays. Guests are welcomed to bring their dogs, children, and their own food and enjoy the outdoor seating with ax throwing, cornhole, and fire pits. Their award-winning spirits are served in imported Scottish Wee Glencairn glassware.

Products:

- Oloroso Sherry Barreled Single Aged malt—four-year-old Single Malt whiskey finished in a Spanish Oloroso barrel, creating a deliciously layered and complex spirit with subtle notes of apricot, toffee, pecans, chocolate, and rich malt

- Strawberry Rhubarb Vodka—created with fresh Oregon strawberries from the Guillermo Family Farm in Amity; fresh rhubarb added for tartness and complexity, and orange peel to round it all out

- Madeira Barrel Aged Rye—eight-year-old rye mash whiskey finished in a Spanish Madeira barrel, creating a deliciously layered and complex spirit with subtle notes of honey, chocolate, caramel, and rye spice

- Club Choice #1 Blended Wheat Whiskey—a Whiskey Club-curated blend of Five-year-old 95% Wheat Whiskey (71 percent of blend); Three-year-old 100% Malted Wheat Whiskey (4 percent); Three-year-old 95% Rye Whiskey (17 percent); Five-year-old 99% Corn Whiskey (4 percent); and Eight-year-old 95% Rye Mash Whiskey (4 percent)

- Cask-Strength 7-Year-Old Reserve Rye—exceptionally smooth and soft mouthfeel; a very small blend of two favorite rye mash whiskey barrels that is superb in cocktails

- Pinot Barrel Aged Malt—single malt whiskey finished in local Pinot Noir barrels; cherry, plum, and wood notes with hints of grass and hay on the nose; blackberry jam, earthy, and light notes of oak on the palate with a smooth finish

- Cask Strength Bourbon—for the whiskey aficionado, a bold, full-strength spirit with notes of butter, caramel, vanilla, oak, and a hint of dark cherries; toffee and lingering heat on the finish

- Oak Bourbon—a classic rye-forward bourbon that balances sweet notes with the spice from the rye; creamy mouthfeel, sweet vanilla caramel, cinnamon, rye spicey, and a hint of cherry

- Russet Potato Vodka—made from 100 perent Idaho russet potatoes with exceptionally smooth and soft mouthfeel; very subtle earthy notes shine through. Gluten-free

- Burnishes Vodka—very smooth corn vodka as it is burnished—treated with a patented process that removes many of the bad, hangover-inducing alcohols that are created during distillation

Freeland Spirits

Portland, Oregon

Freeland Spirits is female-founded and female-crafted - one of the few women-owned distilleries in the country. Inspired by her grandmother, Meemaw Freeland, owner Jill Kuehler applied her passion for agriculture to making quality booze. She has planted community gardens in Guatemala; worked as a farmhand in Port Angeles; and run a non-profit farm in Portland. She also really loves whiskey.

One fateful evening in 2016, Jill was throwing back whiskey with her good friend Corrie, who raises grass-fed beef in Eastern Oregon. When Jill shared her dream of starting a distillery, her friend confided that she'd always wanted to produce grain on the ranch. If you make it, I'll grow it, Corrie said. And with that, Freeland Spirits was born. Today, Jill continues to honor her grandmother's memory by incorporating Oregon's rich bounty of grains and produce into our handcrafted spirits. And just like Meemaw, she continues to blaze her own trail.

Master Distiller Molly Troupe "commands perfection with every spirit she crafts." As the distillery says, "Fun fact—*women have more taste buds and 50 percent more olfactory cells than their male counterparts. In other words, you want a woman making your spirits.*" Molly's background in chemistry pairs well with her education in distillation (completed in Scotland). Their cold distillation process preserves the tasting notes of their unique spirits:

Our fresh flavors come from a process like no other. Our traditional copper pot still, lovingly named Hellbitch, works alongside our singular and best-in-class cold vacuum macerator.

This dual distillation yields gins that are brighter and more vibrant, and allows us to use fresh ingredients in the distillation process. Fresh herbs would be cooked and die in traditional distilling, so most commercially produced gins are made with essences. But with our process, the delicate flavors of our "fresh five" botanicals are maintained, resulting in gin that is beautifully fragrant and delicious to sip neat or mix up in your favorite cocktail.

Check out their tasting room in Northwest Portland, where visitors are greeted with heaters and blankets during the unforgiving PNW winter. They offer a fantastic cocktail program featuring their spirits—Old Fashioneds, Apricot Gimlets, Aperol Collins, Spiced Pear Fizzes, Negronis, and Blackberry Brambles

are always on the menu. Tasting flights, distillery tours, snacks, and paninis are available as well. Feel free to bring the kiddos and doggos, and grab one of their beautiful unique glass bottles of gin or award-winning whiskey on your way out.

Products:

- Gin—a sensory journey with zesty citrus, garden herbs, and warm spice with woodsy notes of juniper and spruce; expertly distilled using a dual distillation process; their "fresh five" botanicals—rosemary, mint, cucumber, thyme, and honey—play nicely with 14 dried botanicals

- Dry Gin—clocks in at 57 percent alcohol because strong women deserve strong gin; packed with bold juniper flavor, with notes of pine forest, mulled spices, green olive, and a hint of citrus

- Bourbon—evokes memories of a Southern kitchen, with soft caramel and baked berries layered with vanilla beans, cocoa, and spice; rested in Oregon pinot noir oak barrels

Hood River Distillers

Hood River, Oregon

The Northwest's largest and oldest distillery, Hood River Distillers, has been rooted in Oregon since 1934. They began it all by making fruit wines and brandies from the apples and pears that were going to waste as excess production from the valley's abundant harvests. Located along the Columbia River with majestic Mount Hood as its backdrop, Hood River Distillers has been at its current bottling facility in Hood River since 1969. Created in the PNW, they have expanded significantly over the decades and now produce close to one million cases per year.

Distilleries:

Big Gin Distillery
Home of Big Gin, the Big Gin Distillery joined the Hood River Distillers family in 2016 and is located in Seattle, Washington. "Crafted by bartenders, for bartenders, and designed with old-time ginners and true beginners in mind, there's something for everyone in every sip," they say, proudly.

It all started with founder and third-generation distiller, Ben Capdevielle, who distilled gin as a hobby with his father, "Big Jim." After spending a decade in kitchens and slinging drinks, Ben started making Big Gin, named for his father. Today, Head Distiller Alex Myers now carries on Ben's legacy.

Products:

- Big Gin—Tasmanian pepperberry, cardamom, and cassia with the sweetness of angelica; bright citrus aromas

- Bourbon Barreled Big Gin—rested for six months in once-used bourbon barrels from Heaven Hill Distillery, enriched with flavors of vanilla, charred oak, and tannins

- Peat Barreled Big Gin—aged in both Ardbeg and Laphroaig barrels, creating a unique flavor profile that peat lends

Clear Creek Distillery

Established in 1985, Clear Creek Distillery's driving principle is "to use the bountiful fruits of the Pacific Northwest to create fruit-based spirits that rivaled the best of their European counterparts."

Using old-world techniques and sourcing ingredients from the local orchards and fresh water springs of Mount Hood in the Oregon countryside, Clear Creek is one of the first craft distilleries in the United States. They joined the Hood River Distillers family in 2014 and are currently led by Master Distiller Joseph O'Sullivan and Head Distiller Caitlin Bartelmay.

Products:

- Clear Brandies—*The clear fruit brandies of France—eaux-de-vie—translates to "water of life." Normally bottled at around 80 proof, these spirits are typically served at the end of a meal, or between courses, as a digestif. These spirits are traditionally un-aged to maintain the magnificent intensity and character of the featured fruit. Fruit brandies comprise the heart of Clear Creek, which are produced according to old-world techniques redundant, since "old-world" = traditional European. They use only pure, whole Pacific Northwest-grown fruit. Twenty pounds of pears are purposed for just one 750 ml bottle of their flagship Pear Brandy*

- Grappa—*Grappa is the clear brandy distilled from pressed grapes—also called pomace—a resourceful production that uses a winemaker's discards (skins, stems, and seeds) shoveled by hand into pot stills. Like wine, grappa can vary widely depending on the quality and variety of grape and the techniques used to make it. In Italy it is traditional to serve grappa at the end of a meal where it is thought to aid in digestion*

Ransom Spirits

Sheridan, Oregon

Raised on a farm in upstate New York, Ransom Spirits founder Tad Seestedt "tried his hand at New York City living and corporate America and quickly realized that he missed the farm." So he took the 2,000 mile journey west, finding his way on the Oregon Trail to a farm in Sheridan where he laid the foundation for a winery and distillery.

In 1997, Tad started distilling and single-handedly revived the 18th-century 'Old Tom' Gin process of barrel aging. He also maxed out his credit cards to pay for the project. "With the bank holding him 'Ransom' to pay back his debt," the company says, "he thought the name appropriate for his continued pursuit."

We distill our spirits in a hand-hammered, direct-fired French alembic pot still. We make all of the selective cuts by taste and smell—without the use of robots. Traditional distillation retains greater aromatic intensity and body from the raw materials we select with great care. We mash and ferment our base wort on site weekly in small batches, sourcing local and organic grains where possible and incorporating barley grown on our own farm.

Head Distiller Matt Cechovic, Tad's apprentice, took the reins on harvesting, production, aging, and bottling in 2021. They operate the distillery on six fundamental principles:

1. Don't cut corners
2. Farm everything organically
3. Be good earthlings—stewards of the land (reuse and recycle)
4. Be unique—using unconventional methods
5. Be meticulous—hands-on (no robots) and focus on small batch production
6. Celebrate life in good health and good spirits

Products:

- Bourbon—aged a minimum of two years in charred American oak, including 12-year-old barrels from our French alembic pot stills; rich and warm flavors that balance a soft oak influence and cereal grain with additional hints of cocoa powder, anise, and a deep honey mouthfeel

- Dry Gin—a highly aromatic gin with the most compelling attributes of both genever and dry gin styles; fashioned after Holland's renowned malt wine genevers, combining the maltiness and hop aromas of the style with a decidedly more intense botanical infusion and the iconic Oregon marionberry and local hops

- Hi-Falutin' WhipperSnapper Whiskey—warm, toasty notes of hazelnut and rye loaf, underpinned by creamy malt aromas; lively and giving palate, with a deft balance between aromatics of grain and barrel; notes of crystal malt, demerara sugar, and sweet earth

- Old Tom Gin—subtle maltiness resulting from its base wort of malted barley, combined with an infusion of botanicals in high-proof corn spirits This gin is an historically accurate revival of the predominant spirit in fashion during the mid-1800s, the golden age of American cocktails. The recipe was developed in collaboration with historian, author, and mixologist extraordinaire David Wondrich. Old Tom is the gin for mixing classic cocktails dating from the days before Prohibition

BEER

Fremont Brewing

Georgetown Brewing Co.

CIDER

Locust Cider

Incline Cider Company

Liberty Ciderworks

WINE

Chateau Ste. Michelle Winery

Côte Bonneville and DuBrul Vineyard

Sparkman Cellars

Treveri Cellars

Bionic Wines

SPIRITS

OOLA Distillery

Copperworks Distilling Company

Black Rock Spirits

Dry Fly Distilling

Unicorn Distillery

WASHINGTON

WOODINVILLE

GIG HARBOR

SEATTLE

TACOMA

SPOKANE

YAKIMA

WALLA WALLA

WASHINGTON

THE CITIZENS of the Evergreen State craft some of the best booze on the planet, and it's no mystery why—they grow the finest produce thanks to pristine water. Renowned apples, hops aplenty, and tasty grapes are the perfect inputs for our storied craftspeople to fashion the ciders, wines, brews, and aqua vitae that keep America buzzing. The Cascade Mountains bifurcate the region, providing two distinct climates that are each spectacular for booze production.

WASHINGTON
BEER
—

The craft beer boom in Washington officially began in the 1980s, though its origins can be traced to early hop farms that were first planted here over a hundred years ago. It's a saga that involves an old transmission repair shop in a quiet Seattle neighborhood, a colorful Scotsman from Yakima, and a visionary entrepreneur who led an entire region to develop new tastes for unique varieties of beer. Liquor laws stretching back to the Prohibition era played a key role in the timing of some of these events, though the path was later paved by local breweries that were known for doing things just a little differently. It is an industry that continues to evolve, with new craft breweries opening across the state on an ongoing basis.
—Brad Holden, author of *Seattle Prohibition: Bootleggers,*
Rumrunners, and Graft in the Queen City

It all started with hops. They were brought to the PNW by Ezra Meeker, who was gifted some cuttings by a friend and planted them on his Puyallup Valley farm at the end of the Civil War. His father aided in the harvest of what became Washington's first crop of commercial hops. Word of its profitability spread like kudzu, and it was soon the Valley's largest cash crop, minting Ezra as "The Hop King," a wealthy man within a decade. He opened a shop in London to export hops onto the world market.

At the same time, Charles Carpenter was planting hop cuttings from New York on his land to the east in the Yakima Valley. Carpenter soon realized that the sunny climate and fertile soil on the other side of the Cascades was superb for agriculture, and within ten years he too found himself a hop baron, putting the region on the map as the world's premier producer. He also found himself in fortunate circumstances when Meeker's (and everyone else's) crops to the west were devastated by the hop louse aphid; the sunshine in the east protected their plants from the infestation. Puyallup production never recovered, and Yakima became the undisputed hop center of the world.

Within two decades, Washington's working-class demography was patronizing three large breweries: Seattle Brewing & Malting Company, The Capital Brewing Company, and Schade Brewery in Spokane. SBMC was soon challenging the dominance of St. Louis as the largest brewing enterprise in the West. Washington State, however—always a weather vane to the cultural pulse of the nation—was captured by the temperance movement and banned all alcohol manufacture and sales in November of 1914, a full four years before the nation ratified Prohibition with the 18th Amendment. During the 17-year dry spell, "malt kits"—all the ingredients required to brew beer at home—would become popular with those seeking to bypass the imposed morality, an ode to the technical ingenuity of the Evergreen State's population.

After repeal in 1933, the Washington State Liquor Control Board was assembled to monitor alcohol production and sales in the state (one of their first acts was to impose regulations on the ABV of beer and wine, capping it at an uninspiring 4 percent). SBMC was purchased by local brewer Emil Sick, who also purchased the rights to produce the now-iconic Rainier Beer. His marketing acumen fostered the brand to exponential growth, from a local favorite to regional treasure. Charles Finkel, who began his work with Chateau Ste. Michelle winery, became enamored with European beer and launched Merchant du Vin, a wine and beer importer in Seattle. His influence is credited with exposing Washington beer drinkers (and homebrewers) to more flavorful brews than the popular local lagers and diversifying the state's craft beer scene into a present-day powerhouse. The final pieces of the puzzle were laid when Jimmy Carter signed HR 1337 into law legalizing homebrewing in 1978, which persuaded the WSLCB to loosen its regulations, allowing for beer ABVs of up to 8 percent. (Woo-hoo!)

In 1982, Scottish beer enthusiast Bert Grant launched Grant's Pub, the state's first combination brewery and pub—the brewpub—since Prohibition. He is credited with producing the state's first IPA in 1983, which surged in popularity up and down the entire west coast. The rest, as they say, is history.

Washington Brewers Guild

—

I like to believe that the Northwest was (and still is) a hotbed for craft beer because we have a greater appreciation for life's finer things, but that really isn't true and I know it. It just sounds good.
– Kendall Jones, Washington Beer Blog

FOUNDED IN 1999, the Washington Brewers Guild has a proud history of getting things done for Washington brewers. Working in both Olympia and Washington, D.C., they are committed to representing all brewers, big and small. Their advocacy was instrumental in allowing growlers to be sold through restaurants and grocery stores, self-distribution, and farmers markets (an essential part of PNW culture!).

The Guild is also directly responsible for the creation of the Washington Beer Commission, the only state beer commission in the United States. Their mission? *To promote Washington beer, benefit the state's breweries, and increase awareness and demand.* The organization is allowed 12 brewery festivals per year, the proceeds of which go right back into promotion and marketing of Washington producers. The state now boasts over 240 breweries!

Fremont Brewing

Seattle, Washington

When imagining what type of person opens up a brewery, one likely conjures images of burly bearded men with barrel chests wiping foam from their mustaches and singing drinking songs while toiling over mash. This could not be further from the truth at Fremont Brewery in Seattle. Founder Matt Lincecum is a former attorney specializing in beverage and hospitality law, and founder Sara Nelson is a Ph.D. in cultural anthropology. Founded in 2009, Fremont is a family-owned iconic brand in the Emerald City, located just down the street from the University of Washington. It would be rare to walk into any Seattle bar and not find at least one Fremont brew on tap, and rarer still to find an empty spot on their patio during a sunny summer day.

Fremont began in a 30-barrel brewhouse (Fremont East), and has since expanded to an 80,000-square-foot location with an 80-barrel, three-vessel steam-powered brewing system at their Urban Beer Garden where one can find tasting flights, their special Brewers Reserve product line, NA beverages, a nitro on-tap, and "guest" ciders. The brand is synonymous with Seattle—their logo is the great blue heron, the city's official bird. During my time at UW, I would take jogs west down the water and marvel at their perennially packed taproom filled with activity and chatter. In most local grocery stores in the beer aisle, you will find national brands on the left and local brands on the right, where Fremont beers occupy prime real estate.

Sustainability is front and center in Fremont's ethos and production, for which they have garnered multiple awards from Seattle organizations over the years. They utilize on-site generated steam to power their brewery, water metering and sloped floors to conserve H_2O use, and even capture the heat from their brew kettles for use in their hot water tanks. Energy-saving LED lighting illuminates the space. They are passionate about packaging their products in aluminum cans only, which employ far more recycled materials than glass and require much less CO_2 to transport because of their lighter weight. Their Cowiche Canyon Organic Fresh Hop Ale was the first beer in Washington State to be certified Salmon-Safe, and they partnered with the American Organic Hop Grower Association to lobby for organic hops to be required for organic certification.

Products:

Year-Round Staples

- Lush IPA—medium sweetness with grass and melon notes
- Interurban IPA—Northwest Pale malt, slight bitterness, with piney hops and grapefruit
- Golden Pilsner—crisp and light with honey and and lemon notes
- Dark Star Imperial Oatmeal Stout—black, thick-bodied with chocolate and coffee notes

Barrel-Aged Series

- B-Bomb Bourbon Barrel Aged Imperial Winter Ale—blend of oak barrel-aged ale with notes of leather, toffee, and cacao
- "B-Bads" Oatmeal Stout—smooth oats with chocolate and roasted malts
- The Rusty Nail Imperial Stout—oatmeal stout with licorice and cinnamon bark

Seasonal

- Gose Sour Ale—cucumber and sea salt (August to October)
- Summer Pale Ale—sweet orange and melon flavors (May to September)
- Field to Ferment Fresh Hop Pale Ale—piney hops and mild sweetness (September)
- Imperial Winter Ale—graham cracker, dried fruit, and toffee (November and December)
- Head Full of Dynomite (HFOD)—unique series of ever-changing hazy IPAs

Matt Lincecum

FREMONT BREWING
SEATTLE, WASHINGTON

What does it mean to you to be part of the Seattle brewing community?

The Seattle brewing community is filled with passion, dedication to craft, a general willingness to help each other, and a desire to see each other succeed. To be a part of this community for so long at this point is still exciting and never taken for granted. It also means rarely paying for beer and having access to the world's freshest hops, so that's awesome as well.

What do you wish that people knew about running a brewery?

Nothing really. The business of beer is just like any business. By the time someone has a Fremont beer in their hand, they're relaxing after their job is done. So, I want them to relax, enjoy the beer.

Any mistakes—trial and error—when you first started Fremont?

Started? Mistakes are a part of every day. Fixing them is what sets apart the professionals from the posers.

What's your favorite type of beer?

The one in my hand. If it's a Lush IPA or a Golden Pilsner, that's a good thing because I drink Lush and Golden more than any other beer.

What do you want visitors to experience when they come to Fremont?

Community, quality, hospitality, and the thrill of being around a genuinely good group of your neighbors and friends.

Any weird/crazy/interesting stories from operating a brewery?

None that got past my attorney. If there was one story that could fit through the teeny window of what is appropriate to share with the public, it would definitely be around the sheer joy and awe of our Field to Ferment Fresh Hop beer production. If you can imagine the smell of a freshly picked hop field, the excitement of running on a harvest-dependent schedule for six weeks and close to 50,000 pounds of plump, wet, fresh hops coming in, being put into the kettle, pushed out to our trailer, and smelling like heaven on earth, then that would be a cool story to share. The rest? Well, if you weren't there, you should have been. Good times.

Georgetown Brewing Co.

Seattle, Washington

Two guys that liked beer a lot and hated working for other people came together to start a brewery. Between the time they brewed test batches of pale ales and purchased a 15-barrel system from a defunct brewery in North Carolina in 2002, to now when they support over 70 employees and are the largest independent brewery in Washington State, a lot has happened. How about you come down to the brewery and we'll tell you all about it over some beer?
–Georgetownbeer.com

"Little hand says it's time to rock and roll."
–Bodhi, *Point Break*

Georgetown Brewing started off in the Canary Islands. That's where founder Manuel "Manny" Chao was raised by Chinese and Taiwanese immigrants, who worked in the restaurant industry. They moved to the United States in 1978 so the father could launch new restaurants in New England. After returning from a visit to Portland, Oregon, Dad told his family to pack up once again, as they were relocating to Beaverton. Manny landed a paid internship at Nike (he admittedly spent most of his earnings on Nike gear to outfit himself), on his way to study business at the University of Washington in Seattle. As an underage student at a local watering hole, Manny used a fake ID (his older brother's) to order his very first beer (a porter). That moment is when the real story begins.

Manny was hooked on craft beer. He sought out local draft brews at bars around town, going so far as to keep a diary of tasting notes. His affection for the industry led him to cross paths with Jack Schropp, who was brewing his own stuff in his garage. Manny pestered Jack for months for a job, until he finally caved and offered him a sales position with Mac & Jack's Brewing, slinging their product to local bars and delivering the keg orders.

Manny left Seattle for Mexico, and upon his return, he and his roommate, Roger Bialous, set out to make a hoppy, crisp pale ale that Seattleites would love. After a few tries, they decided upon a recipe that satiated their taste buds, and Manny's Pale Ale was born. They bought a used brewing system, set up shop in the Seattle Brewing building (home to Rainier), and the rest is history. As Roger puts it, "People would try it, and you'd watch their eyes get big as the hop flavor hit their palate. They'd swallow and they'd be like, 'Oh, that's weird, I got a hop flavor without the bitterness.'"

Today, visitors can check out their massive brewery and tasting room in the Georgetown neighborhood, just south of downtown, where they fill thousands of growlers a week. (Give yourself extra time if it's a Seahawks gameday!) Families and well-behaved dogs are welcome. As advocates for the neighborhood—a working-class, semi-industrial landscape filled with incredible bars and restaurants—Manny and Roger encourage guests to have a pint at their tasting room and then head over to other nearby establishments and enjoy their Pale Ale, Roger's Pilsner, and *Point Break*–inspired brews (they are obsessed with the 1991 Keanu Reeves movie) on tap.

The great thing about Seattle is that you can even go into a bad bar, a bar where you wouldn't expect to find good craft beer, and you find good craft beer. And that beer is usually Manny's.
– Seattle Beer News Blog

Products:

- Manny's Pale Ale—the OG, a rich and complex malty middle with a snappy hop finish; crisp, clean, and smooth with hints of citrus and fruit

- Roger's Pilsner—refreshing pilsner with a spicy and earthy hop aroma

- Lucille IPA—floral, citrusy, and awesome; anything so innocent and built like that's just gotta be named Lucille

- Johnny Utah Pale Ale—heavy grapefruit, citrus, and resin in the nose, with minimal malt interference, giving the beer a clean finish without a cloying bitterness

- Bodhizafa IPA—light, silky texture with flavor and aroma both expressing mandarin and citrus all around

WASHINGTON
CIDER

—

Locust Cider

Gig Harbor, Washington

 Another successful enterprise run by brothers, Jason and Patrick Spears founded Locust in 2015, specializing in modern ciders. Things escalated quickly, and visitors can now enjoy their products in 13 Washington locations, from Alki Beach to Woodinville and everywhere in between.

Our goal is to make ciders that don't just make you say, "Yum, that's good." We want to make you say, "Hell yeah, that's amazing!" We are not beholden to tradition, but we respect it. We love nurturing unique apple varieties to deliver the best traditional dry ciders possible. But we also love getting crazy and using the common Washington eating apple as a vehicle to create flavor combinations that make you say, "Hell Yeah!"

Products:

- Blackberry Cider—dry, complex, and tart cider made from Washington apples and blackberries

- Cold Pressed Apple Cider—perfectly balanced with cold pressed apples

- Dark Cherry Cider—Washington apples blended with sweet dark Bing cherries; slightly tart, barely sweet, with fresh cherry flavor

- Juicy Peach Cider—Washington apples blended with peach juice for a peach-forward experience

- Berry Blues Cider—Washington apples blended with blueberry, hibiscus, and vanilla; light bodied with a blueberry flavor and a lot of underlying complexity

- Bourbon Barrel Aged Orange Blossom—Washington apples aged in Bourbon barrels blended with orange and cherry, just like an Old Fashioned

- Cold Brew Coffee—a surprisingly balanced hard cider featuring Cutters Point Cold Brew Coffee and cider made from WA apples; notes of toasted mallow, baker's chocolate, amaretto, and light spice balanced with hazelnut and vanilla for a super smooth finish

Incline Cider Company

Tacoma, Washington

Incline Cider Company was built by the father and son team Chris and Jordan Zehner in 2015, with a mission to share quality craft cider with the world. Their innovative brews use fresh-pressed Washington apples from Yakima, never too dry nor too sweet, always vegan and gluten-free. You can find the pair pouring cider alongside their wives at local brewfests and also at their Tacoma taproom.

Products:

- Hopped—lightly dry-hopped with a blend of Citra, Cascade, and Galaxy hops to pull out citrus aromas; balanced, bright, refreshing, and certainly not too sweet

- Marionberry—the cabernet of the blackberry family pours a dark purple with an inviting dark fruit nose; fruit forward with a tart finish that keeps it balanced

- Blood Orange—juicy blood orange and citrus notes with a touch of tart to keep things balanced

- Imperial Hazy Honeycrisp—hazy, bold, and refreshing, crafted with the famous Honeycrisp apple, with notes of citrus, honey, and light spice

- Imperial Tart Cherry—full of cherry notes while remaining perfectly balanced, with a finish on the drier and more crisp side

- Strawberry Sea—notes of ripe, fresh strawberries balanced by a crisp, refreshing finish

- Prickly Pear—tropical aromas and a vibrant fuchsia color accent the unique characteristics of the cactus fruit; tropical, earthy, bright, and semi-dry

- Beare's Original Haze—crisp apple flavor while being on the sessionable side at 5 percent ABV, showcasing the famous Honeycrisp apple, with notes of citrus, honey, and a hint of orange

Liberty Ciderworks

Spokane, Washington

Liberty was founded in 2013 by Rick Hastings and Austin Dickey, who met while working at the same architectural firm. Austin discovered cider while touring as a student in the UK, and it became a hobby. Rick unlocked his affinity for cider courtesy of his gluten-intolerant brother, and began making it, too—through close book research, visits to regional cideries, and classes led by international cider expert Peter Mitchell, all with an eye towards opening an urban cidery someday. In 2019, two regular customers, Ben and Jamie Pratt, assumed Austin's place and now lead sales and management for Liberty. Last year, Jamie became Washington State's first Certified Pommelier, a title analogous to sommelier (wine) or cicerone (beer).

"Even in the 'Apple State' of Washington, people are still discovering cider, and we've found having a tasting room is essential to showcasing the depth and variety fine cider can offer," Rick says. "Besides our own products, we maintain a curated selection of ciders from the Northwest and around the globe, including French, U.K., and Spanish styles, perries (pear ciders), pommeaus (brandy fortified ciders), ice ciders, and more.

"We've lived in and been fans of Spokane for decades, and we are excited to be a part of its growth as a food and beverage destination. We're extremely fortunate to have found three local orchards to supply all our apples, each growing cider-specific varieties in much the same way as vintners grow grapes. We've been deliberate in making cider that reflects local soils and growing conditions—using only apples that thrive here plus the native yeast found in each orchard. Our collective efforts have made Liberty one of the most influential and highly-regarded cideries in the region."

Products:

- Sixpenny—crisp pineapple, stone-fruit, and honey aromas and flavors

- Wickson Crabapple—grape, pineapple, lychee, and honey notes, with a white pepper and mildly tannic finish

- 55 Chain—Made in the U.K. "West Country" style, featuring tannic English varietals (Dabinett, Chisel Jersey, and Brown's apples), native yeast, oak barrels, and lots of time

- Splintercat—made from Dolgo crabapples and honey, sweet with a tart, crabapple finish; rich and full-bodied, with berry notes, citrus bite, and unmistakable honey character

WASHINGTON
WINE

—

Washington wine's earliest days date back to 1825, when the first grapevines were planted. While history made us, we're now making history. Get to know where we've been, so you understand where we're going.
—Washington State Wine Commission

Fort Vancouver, on the mighty Columbia River, is the genesis of the Washington wine industry. Using English seeds, the Hudson's Bay Company first planted grapes here in 1825. Their agriculture spread to the Walla Walla Valley just before the Civil War. In 1902, William Bridgman arrived in Sunnyside and introduced large-scale irrigation, sourcing the waters of snowcap runoff from the encompassing Cascades. His lasting contribution was grapes; an acre of Sunnyside still to this day boasts an acre of Thompson Seedless and Muscat vines that he planted in 1917. Within just a few years, Eastern Washington was throwing its inaugural Columbia River Valley Grape Carnival.

Like it did to everything else fun, Prohibition put the kibosh on grape production in 1920. After what was likely a very boring 13 years, Congress repealed the law and Washington State embraced booze once again by creating the state's Liquor Control Board. In 1934, Bridgman launched Upland Winery, which lasted into the 1960s. Local growers formed the Washington State Wine Commission in 1935, as the few dozen wineries that existed at the time began ramping up production once again. Cabernet sauvignon was first planted in the 1940s and 1950s. The vines at Otis Vineyard in Yakima are now some of the oldest in the country. Over the next decade, Washington State University (WSU) began establishing programs for viticulture, enology, and irrigation, as riesling grapes were introduced and chardonnay and merlot arrived. Soon after, some of Washington's most revered and iconic vineyards were established: Ste. Michelle, Harrison Hill, Cold Creek, Celilo, and Red Willow. The *Los Angeles Times* held a blind taste test of rieslings in 1974 and Chateau Ste. Michelle won top prize, gaining it and the region national prominence.

If Bridgman is the godfather of Washington wine, then Walter Clore is its Michael Corleone. A researcher, he arrived at Washington State University's agricultural outpost in Prosser in 1937. Bridgman gifted Clore some vines, leaving him fascinated with the prospect of making wine. As overseer of WSU's viticultural research, he was directly responsible for planting over 300 grape varieties, in addition to his innovations in trellis design that led to new mechanical harvesting techniques. He was named Man of the Year by the Washington State Grape Society in 1997. A scholarship in his honor is awarded to this day at the University.

The federal government approved Yakima Valley as the state's first American Viticultural Area (AVA) in 1983, as Washington established itself as the second-largest producer of wines behind California. Then came the Columbia Valley AVA, Puget Sound AVA, Columbia Gorge AVA—now numbering 20 in the present day. The year 2000 is known as "The Big Bang," when wine production and consumption boomed. By the end of the decade, there were nearly 450 licensed wineries in the state. Around 2012, red wine overtook white wine in production, as cabernet surpassed riesling and chardonnay.

In 2023, the Evergreen State boasted over 1,000 thriving wineries.

Chateau Ste. Michelle Winery

Woodinville, Washington

Our winemaking philosophy is to highlight the style, quality, and expression of our Washington state vineyards. We strive to respect the varietal characters and individuality of each location, yet still craft each wine to give you a pleasurable, food-friendly experience. From crisp, refreshing rieslings to elegant, complex chardonnays and from powerful Cold Creek Cabernet Sauvignon to restrained Canoe Ridge Merlot, our wines show individuality, with a stamp of softness and approachability that we work on at every step of the winemaking process.
–www.ste-michelle.com

Chateau Ste. Michelle Winery, celebrating over 50 years of production, actually comprises two state-of-the-art facilities and three vineyards. Its whites are produced at the Chateau in Woodinville, Washington, home of the tasting room and Summer Concert Series. Its reds are produced on the other side of the Cascade Mountains in the Columbia Valley, where Ste. Michelle owns 3,500 acres of vineyards over three estates: Cold Creek Vineyard, Horse Heaven Vineyard, and Canoe Ridge Estate.

All of their grapes are sourced within the Columbia Valley AVA. The mountains form a blockade around Western Washington's wet, Pacific-driven climate, limiting annual rainfall in the east to eight inches. All vines in the AVA are planted on their own rootstock (as Phylloxera, the root-eating aphid, is not a threat), preserving the varietals' characteristics and extending the longevity of the vineyards. Here, sunny skies bring temperatures into the mid-80s during the summer, while cooler autumnal weather provides excellent ripening conditions and protects the grapes' natural acidity. The result is intense, distinct aromas and flavors, making this region's wines some of America's best.

Horse Heaven Vineyard was planted in the early 1980s, and the appellation was officially declared an AVA as Horse Heaven Hills in 2005. Its warm summers, low rainfall, and temperature moderation by the adjacent Columbia River provide perfect growing conditions for chenin blanc and sauvignon blanc, mostly on southern-facing slopes of quick-draining, sandy silt-loam soil sitting atop volcanic basalt. High winds create resilient grapes resistant to mold and pests. The climate allows for later harvesting, leading to more uniform ripening.

Canoe Ridge Estate comprises 559 acres of the Horse Heaven Hills AVA, planted in 1991. The terrain was carved 12 million years ago by lava flows, leaving behind basalt in its path. More recently (13,000 years ago), the last ice age deposited nutrient-rich soils, sandy loam with cobblestone. Ste. Michelle grows their cabernet sauvignon, chardonnay, merlot, and syrahs here, the warm climate encouraging these classic varieties. Ste. Michelle executes all of its production of reds here.

The iconic Cold Creek Vineyard was planted in 1973 with cabernet franc, cabernet sauvignon, chardonnay, merlot, and riesling. It began as a hayfield, and when Ste. Michelle planted the 500+ acres, they immediately doubled the state's grape production. Its microclimate is one of the warmest in the state, and the low rainfall allows for controlled irrigation - two factors that contribute to the grapes' intensity, color, and flavor concentration. You can expect "big-shouldered" reds and crisp, robust whites from this area.

The Chateau northeast of Seattle is the prime destination for boozy travelers to Woodinville wine country. The Chateau Kitchen offers charcuterie, flatbreads, and paninis to stabilize your day drinking. They offer tours of the estate, blending classes, and even a "Black Glass" blind tasting experience. Guests can reserve featured flight tastings and then head outside to enjoy bottles and appetizers in private igloos (the weather be damned). For weekend visitors, they offer their Weekend Brunch Box Experience with house sparkling wine, fresh juices, and paired food offerings. For connoisseurs, the Library Wine Tasting is especially tantalizing - guests can savor their private stock of the very last of vintages. Summer visitors are encouraged to align their travel plans with Ste. Michelle's Concert Series calendar. Their amphitheater has hosted big-name acts since 1984 like the Beach Boys, James Taylor, Sheryl Crow, John Legend, and local icon Dave Matthews. Grab a bottle and a beach chair and enjoy the show!

Products:

Collaborations

- Eroica—German Winemaker Ernst Loosen uses Washington grapes to create a beautifully acidic riesling
- Col Solare—Tuscan Winemaker Marchesi Antinori crafts a renowned cabernet sauvignon–dominate blend with grapes from the Red Mountain AVA

Whites

- 2021 Sauvignon Blanc (Horse Heaven Hills)—grapefruit and honeysuckle
- 2022 Indian Wells Riesling—stone fruit and crisp citrus
- 2021 Mimi Chardonnay—lightly oaked, bright taste
- Luxe Brut Rosé—strawberries, sweet orange, and berry jam
- 2017 Ethos Reserve Late Harvest Muscat—apricot, peaches, baking spice

Reds

- Cabernet Sauvignon (Canoe Ridge Estate)—ripe dark cherries
- Midsummer's Red Blend—Rhône-style, blackberry and raspberry
- Indian Wells Red Blend—boysenberry and biscotti
- Merlot (Canoe Ridge Estate)—silky, elegant tannins
- 2014 Ethos Reserve Syrah—fruity layers and sweet finish

Côte Bonneville and DuBrul Vineyard

Yakima, Washington

Wine grapes are smart. They thrive in great places to live, with beautiful hillsides and nice weather. The Yakima Valley is no exception! It's an amazing place to enjoy the long days of summer. It's similar for the vines – long days mean they bask in the sun, soaking it up for photosynthesis and energy. At this point in the season, the grapes are pea sized, green, and hard, and yet, flavors of the eventual wines are already being determined by the amount of sunlight that they get. As the summer progresses, the light will be important for developing color, flavors, and tannin structure.

So many important details of the vineyard are encapsulated in the location, playing into the importance of terroir. While the word literally means soil, it's not just the soil profile and geologic makeup that matter, but also the aspect, elevation, air drainage, and microclimate. Great terroir grows consistently great fruit. In Washington, higher elevation vineyards mean rockier soils, better air drainage, and protection from winter frost. These things all play into the consistent high quality wines that DuBrul Vineyard is known for.

–Kerry Shiels, winemaker, Côte Bonneville

In 1991, Kathy and Hugh Shiels purchased 45 acres of land in the Yakima Valley, cleared out remnants of the apple orchard that existed there previously, and planted grapes. Those riesling vines are now some of the oldest in Washington State, sold under the label Côte Bonneville since 2001 as wine that showcases the fruit from this land, DuBrul Vineyard. Kathy and Hugh's daughter, Kerry Shiels, earned her master's in Viticulture and Enology from UC Davis and returned to Yakima as Côte Bonneville's winemaker.

This small acreage is unique, consisting of multiple microclimates that can measure just a few hundred feet. For decades they have been working in partnership with Washington State University to study and innovate production techniques, especially with irrigation. They switched from overhead sprinklers to drip water in their deficit irrigation program, an optimization strategy wherein crops are watered only during drought-sensitive growth stages. This sustainable practice combined with their low-vigor soils results in small berries, small clusters, and low yields (but they still manage to output over 2,500 cases per year).

"We are also grateful for the spectacular site that DuBrul Vineyard is planted on. Rocky hillsides are the perfect situation with winter snow. You want the right amount of water in the soil in the spring, when vines are growing quickly. With all the rocks in DuBrul, the snowmelt won't stick around for long. The vines will pick up some of this moisture, but not too much. The rest will flow as groundwater down the valley.

"The other advantage to being high on the hill is that cold air, like water, flows downhill. Extreme cold temperatures can harm the buds that hold the next season's growth. Low spots hold the cold air longer, putting the vines at greater risk for cold damage. DuBrul is high on the hill. There are no spots where cold air is trapped. There is good air drainage to keep everything moving."

Products:

- 2022 Riesling—oldest vines from DuBrul Vineyard

- 2022 Cabernet Franc Rosé—dry, bright acidity and medium-bodied

- 2019 Chardonnay—Sur Lees aging gives unfiltered, creamy texture

- 2020 Train Station Cabernet Franc—only 26 rows of these spicy, bright grapes

- 2018 Carriage House—blend of cab sauv, merlot, and cab franc

Sparkman Cellars

Woodinville, Washington

Before creating Sparkman Cellars, Kelly had a degree in Wildlife Biology, working to rehabilitate peregrine falcons in Wyoming and protecting spotted owls in California. Chris was a National Sea Grant fellow and Peace Corps volunteer, later managing high-end restaurants and named 2010 Sommelier of the Year by *Seattle Magazine*. The Sparkmans—both raised in Tennessee—are a dynamic duo of winemaking here in Woodinville, the wine mecca a short drive east of the Emerald City. Launched in 2004, Sparkman Cellars was awarded #11 in *Wine Spectator's* Top 100 Winemakers (2016). "Family. Good Livin'. Real Fine Wine," they say. "Seems like that makes sense to people. Especially if your wine is delicious and your kids are good people."

In Year One we made one baby girl, 12 barrels of wine and three labels in a tiny warehouse. In Year Three we made another baby girl, opened our first tasting room, made 1,425 cases of wine and eight labels. We have now grown our annual production to over 12,000 cases in our shiny new winery, tasting room, and event hall at the old Redhook Brewery in Woodinville.

Products:

- Kingpin Cabernet Sauvignon—leads with aromas of black fruits, frangipane, mushrooms, sweet oak, minerals, and cigar box coupled with firm, silky tannins that frame rich black cherry, dark chocolate, roasted herbs, and minerals

- Stella Mae Cabernet Sauvignon Blend—nose of forest floor, mushrooms, black tea, iodine, rosemary, blackberry, cedar and mineral

- Ruckus Syrah—built with co-fermented syrah and viognier, and embellished with a sizable dash of cabernet sauvignon; blackberries and blueberries meshed with garrigue, funk, tar, and stone all encased in velvety textural robes

- Apparition Rhône Blend—attacks the nose with exotic Asian spices, paraffin, and almond extract and layers of nectarine, honey, and peachy lychee, finishing with a rich yet clean minerally creaminess

- As You Wish Old Vines Sauvignon Blanc—aromas of honey, fresh flowers, white nectarine, pink grapefruit, melon, and petrichor with flavors of ripe Meyer lemon, guava, crushed stone, jalapeño, and herbes de Provence

- This Old Porch Rosé—bone dry, minerally, and versatile; gushes strawberry, stone fruit, melon, and guava

Treveri Cellars

Yakima, Washington

Treveri's German-born founder and head winemaker, Jürgen Grieb holds degrees in both winemaking and sparkling winemaking. After honing his skills at the Karthäuserhof Winery in the Ruwer Valley and Duhr Sektkellerei (sparkling house), he immigrated to the United States in the early 1980s. His son, Christian, with a childhood spent in the winery, was quick to join the family business—he now works alongside his father as a winemaker and VP of sales.

The Griebs implement the Méthode Traditionnelle used in Champagne, France—the classic sparkling vinification process. This practice yields the highest quality and most complex wines possible, but the trade-off is that it is the most labor intensive, expensive, and time-consuming way to make bubbles, requiring a secondary fermentation to take place inside the bottle, which is temporarily capped after the liqueur de tirage (wine, sugar, and yeast solution) is added to the base wine. When the yeasts have finished working, they die and become lees. Then comes riddling, wherein the sediments are removed by inverting the bottle, trapping and freezing them, then removing the temporary cap so the bottle's pressure forces out the unwanted solids.

Treveri is Washington's most decorated sparkling winemaker—they have nine wines with a score of 90 or above. They produce over 40,000 cases of varietal sparkling per year. Their products have even been served at the White House!

Products:

- Blanc de Blancs Brut Zero—sometimes referred to as "Brut Nature," produced with zero dosage, allowing the wine to ferment with zero residual sugar; hints of citrus and melon with a creamy finish

- Brut Blanc de Noir—the pinot grape adds complexity and depth without adding color, giving the wine special characteristics that set it apart

- Sparkling Rosé—a blend of syrah and chardonnay carefully selected from the Hilltop and Pleasant Vineyards in the Yakima Valley; beautiful color combined with strawberry rhubarb and a bit of yeast on the nose

- Sparkling Gewürztraminer—notes of lychee jelly combined with rich tropical fruit, allspice, nutmeg, and clove, balanced with an underlying acidity

- Sparkling Syrah Brut—deep red color with an effervescence sure to delight, melding dark cherries, tobacco, and spice for a rich, flavorful finish

Bionic Wines

Walla Walla, Washington

Bionic Wines is the family of brands produced by renowned French vigneron (winegrower) Christophe Baron. In 1997, Christophe was the first grower to plant vines in the Stones of the Walla Walla Valley in the Pacific Northwest, a project he named Cayuse Vineyards. In the past 25 years, Cayuse wines have achieved critical acclaim and several 100-point scores from major publications. Christophe's American portfolio has grown to include three other productions: Horsepower Vineyards, Hors Catégorie Vineyards, and No Girls Wines. Christophe also produces Champagne Christophe Baron on his vineyard parcels in the Marne Valley in Champagne, France, where he grew up. Christophe has championed "closed circle" farming since his first vines took root, and in 2002, was the first to implement biodynamic farming techniques in the Walla Walla Valley. In 2008, with Horsepower Vineyards, he became the first vigneron in the United States to create a project dedicated to cultivating vineyards using draft horses (you could not get a tractor in there if you tried)—an effort which revived the methods of traditional agriculture used by his ancestors in their family vineyards. Horsepower Vineyards features high-density, meter-by-meter planting, similar to the approach of some of Christophe's favorite vignerons in the northern Rhône. This choice is a nod, in part, to how his family used to farm; it's also incredibly beneficial for social health, ergo great for producing wines of unparalleled quality.

The Bionic Wines family is connected through Christophe's essential principles of uncompromising quality realized through hard work in the vineyards, a deft touch in the cellar, and an unwavering commitment to his terroirs. The result: distinctive wines of character which allow each site and variety to shine.

Cayuse Vineyards

Founded in 1997, Cayuse grew to encompass five vineyards, comprising almost 45 acres which average a yield of only two tons of grapes per acre and are planted predominantly to syrah, grenache, and tempranillo. Cabernet franc, cabernet sauvignon, merlot, and viognier make up the difference. All Cayuse wines have been produced exclusively with estate-grown fruit since 2000. In 2002, Cayuse became the first Domaine in the Walla Walla Valley to farm exclusively using biodynamic methods.

Horsepower Vineyards

Christophe created Horsepower Vineyards in 2008 as an homage to his family history and traditional old-world farming techniques: draft horses were used on his family's estates in Champagne until 1957 when his grandfather became the first local vigneron to invest in a tractor. Now Christophe is bringing craftsmanship full-circle, eschewing technology for four Belgian and two Percheron draft horses to cultivate 18 acres of vineyards with a connection to the land that has been largely lost with conventional mechanized farming.

Horsepower sources fruit exclusively from four estate vineyards in the Stones of the Walla Walla Valley: Sur Echalas, The Tribe, High Contrast, and Fiddleneck.

Hors Catégorie

When Christophe locked eyes on a dramatic, very steep slope of fragmented basalt on the north fork of the Walla Walla River in 2003, he realized its enormous potential. Surrounded by an abandoned orchard and the wrecks of long-forgotten mobile homes, its aggressively pitched incline and volcanic soils immediately reminded him of syrah's spiritual birthplace: the great vineyards of the northern Rhône Valley. He knew he had found the most challenging project of his career—the opportunity to plant a one-of-a-kind vineyard from scratch.

After purchasing the property in 2005, it took six years to plant the Hors Catégorie Vineyard, named for the French bicycle racing term to designate a climb that is "beyond categorization" and which reaches a grade of almost 60 percent in places.

The first vines, spaced at 3.5-square-foot intervals, went into the ground on April 11, 2011, making Hors Catégorie one of Walla Walla Valley's most densely planted vineyards. The vineyard is so steep that manual labor is the only option: plows are affixed to winches and pulled up the hill in order to cultivate the rocky terrain according to biodynamic methods.

All this sweat and toil results in a wine which takes the esthetics of superlative Rhône syrah, and channels them through the geology, topography, climate, and aspect of this unique site to create what *Wine Spectator's* Harvey Steiman described as one of the great jewels of the wine world, adding, "This combination of expressiveness, power, and weightlessness is rare in American syrah."

An average of 1,800 bottles is created each year. Since 2013, every vintage has been sold exclusively to Hors Catégorie Mailing List members and great restaurants.

No Girls

No girls, only women—because empowered women create empowered wine

The name was inspired by the mid-20th century shuttering of Walla Walla Valley's colorful historic bordellos—previously a notable feature of thriving towns in the American Wild West. When the bordellos closed, the phrase "No Girls" painted on the walls also signified the larger cultural shift toward women's rights and progressive ideas. Christophe named this wine No Girls in celebration of independent, talented women everywhere, including those behind some of the world's greatest wine productions. After working with Christophe on the first two vintages, Cayuse Vineyards Resident Vigneronne Elizabeth Bourcier has independently helmed the wine creation of this project from the 2010 vintage.

No Girls is crafted from grenache, syrah, and tempranillo from the biodynamically farmed La Paciencia Vineyard. *Wine Spectator* called the 2009 vintage of No Girls "some of the best Washington wines ever rated" by the magazine.

Women-Operated Spirit Producers in the Pacific Northwest

—

- Oregon Spirit Distillers (Bend, Oregon)
- Vivacity Spirits (Albany, Oregon)
- Trail Distilling (Oregon City, Oregon)
- Ewing Young Distillery (Newberg, Oregon)
- Wild Roots Spirits (Portland, Oregon)
- The Aimsir Distilling Company (Portland, Oregon)
- Freeland Spirits (Portland, Oregon)
- Stillweather Spirits (Portland, Oregon)
- JAZ Spirits (Albany, Oregon)
- Royalty Spirits (Portland, Oregon)
- BroVo Spirits (Woodinville, Washington)
- Fast Penny Spirits (Seattle, Washington)
- Scratch Distillery (Edmonds, Washington)

WASHINGTON
SPIRITS

—

OOLA Distillery
Seattle, Washington

Kirby Kallas-Lewis is likely not who you have in mind when you envision a master spirits maker. He is tall and thin—not bearded and burly like one might expect—and he is jolly, inviting, and generous. He was born in St. Paul, majored in sculpture and fine art in college, and after school he hitchhiked to Alaska to work on fishing boats. From there he purchased a one-way ticket to the South Pacific and spent the next two decades traveling and living in the region. He is considered one of the most important dealers of South Pacific antiquities in the world. In 2008, he bought a still and set it up in his bathtub at home; within two years, he founded OOLA Distillery, Seattle's oldest maker of spirits.

"We like to say that our product is 'artfully distilled,'" explains Alan Jackson, OOLA's managing director, as he shows me around their operations plant in the industrial SODO (as in "south of the dome") district. They use low-yield yeast, which reduces their output but produces a better-tasting product. Alan explains that they distill "on the grain," meaning that the grain is not separated before fermentation, adding to the texture and the flavor of their spirits. Their bourbon is made using a stainless pot still, and aged in barrels for five and a half years—the longest aging processes of any bourbon made in Seattle—at a facility next to a Buddhist monastery (which Alan credits for an infusion of positive vibes into the barrels). For their gin, Kirby adorns a white lab coat and adds a proprietary blend of 13 botanicals to their neutral vodka spirit, creating a wonderful new-world product that makes an incredible Gin and Tonic. All of their spirits are organic and certified Salmon-Safe, and they recently installed a closed-loop water cooling system that now saves them tens of thousands of gallons of water per year.

Visitors can take distillery tours of their production facility in the Georgetown neighborhood and make reservations for their cocktail classes featuring OOLA spirits.

Products:

- Waitsburg Bourbon—spicy rye base with notes of sweet vanilla, brown sugar, and maple syrup; aged six to eight years

- OOLA Gin—neutral vodka spirit infused with Kirby's secret blend of herbs and spices

- OOLA Vodka—complex and light bodied with cracked pepper bite

SEATTLE, WASHINGTON

COPPERWORKS

DISTILLING COMPANY™

MALT WHISKEY

LOT NO. 2015 F 03 - P
BARREL NO. 92
PROOF 110.0

DSP-WA-21028 • RC 53 G

Copperworks Distilling Company

Seattle, Washington

Jason Parker met me at his distillery near Pike Place Market one after-noon to show me around and tell me the story of Copperworks. I inter-rupted his lunch, and I told him that I had plenty of time and to please enjoy his meal. "No, I'm good!" he exclaimed as he popped up from his desk and enthusi-astically shook my hand. He mentioned that he's from Kentucky, and I excitedly told him that my family was, too. "How did you make it all the way out here to Seattle?"

"I ran out of land getting away from Kentucky," he jokes.

Graduating from Evergreen College after studying chemistry and microbiol-ogy, Jason founded the iconic Pike Brewery in the Market in 1989. "From great brewing comes great spirits," he tells me. The local brewing community came together organically, he explains, with a "really good camaraderie." He would use his brewing knowledge to open Copperworks some years later, with the goal of making high-quality beer, then distilling it. "We are brewers first," he says. "I think brewers and distillers will be interchangeable in 50 years.

"We have never made a decision based on inefficiency," he goes on. "For a distillery, starting with beer is inefficient. It's all about flavor - not yield." Sourc-ing their ingredients from local breweries—Pike, Elysian, and Fremont to name a few—they distill fermented grain and age the spirit in oak barrels. "We didn't need to be traditional," explains Jason, "and that also means removing tradi-tional impurities from our spirits." Copperworks uses a vintage approach to their whiskey making process, meaning they source single-farm malt to infuse individual characteristics to their batches, much like grapes to a winery. As he says, "whiskey is the perfect product for malt!" Their Batch 39 Whiskey was the first such spirit to be certified Salmon-Safe from Washington State, and like OOLA they have installed a towered water-cooling system that now saves them tens of thousands of gallons of water in the production process.

Visitors should check out their tasting room in Downtown Seattle for guided flights and distillery tours. For a special memory, check out their Single Malt Blending Classes, where Jason will guide you through a series of batches from their barrels and send you home with a bottle of your own unique blend that you create.

Products:

- Copperworks American Single-Malt Whiskey—twice-distilled, barrel-aged at least 32 months

- New Oak Cask Finished Gin—Ten botanicals, finished in charred American oak barrels

- Copperworks Plum Gin—limited edition using plums from Warm Valley Orchard

- Copperworks Vodka—malted barley base; great for Moscow Mules

- Copperworks Gin—well-balanced; distilled in Scottish copper

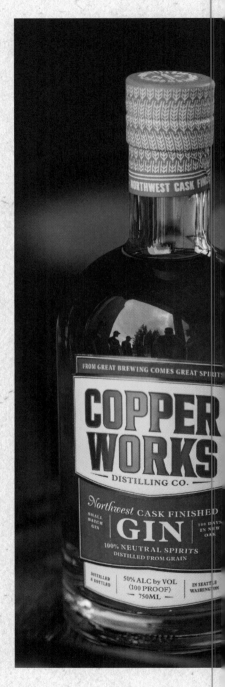

Black Rock Spirits

Seattle, Washington

I first met Sven Liden at my company's five-year anniversary party—we rented their Tequila Lab office near Lumen Field (home to the Seahawks and Sounders) to host the event. The creaky wooden building that houses their headquarters is over a hundred years old, compartmentalized into artist lofts. Sven met me downstairs to let me in so I could set up for the party, and we started talking shop, chatting about booze, bartending, and their old-school office.

"Ya know, this room was Nirvana's first practice space," Sven says nonchalantly.

"What!?" I exclaim. "That's awesome! Our event tonight is a 1990s-themed costume party, how fitting."

"Cool," he says. "Hey, would you guys want to try some of our tequila tonight?"

Yes we would, I nod. Yes we would.

With his partner, Chris Marshall, Sven started Black Rock Spirits in Seattle in 2008. The first they sold was a bottle of Bakon, a bacon-infused vodka designed for the Bloody Mary cocktail, in 2009. "We realized that as a small company, it's very difficult to achieve the reach that big spirits brands get by spending millions of dollars on marketing," says Sven. "Our strategy has been to produce very high-quality products, but to market the bottles and brands in ways that get attention just from the name or label. But, with Bakon, instead of just going

get attention just from the name or label. But, with Bakon, instead of just going for novelty, we decided to use all natural ingredients and a high-quality potato base. In the last decade it's won countless national awards for 'Best Bloody Mary.'

"Most of the time, when you are introduced to a new spirit, it's because a big company paid a distributor sales rep to introduce the product to a bartender, even paid to print their menus and 'featured cocktail' lists," Sven explains. "They just throw a lot of money to push awareness of a new brand. We have always been focused on a 'pull' vs 'push' strategy. We started off with a really attention-getting product, Bakon Vodka—made almost exclusively for Bloody Marys—but our next product, Sparkle Donkey Tequila, is also meant to get attention with unique and funny branding—including a fake documentary about the history of 'El Burro Esparkalo,' a donkey that came down the hillside to deliver tequila to a

town in need. We use very high-quality ingredients and traditional cooking and distillation methods.

"We work with a boutique distillery in the town of Tequila, Mexico, to make a 100 percent agave tequila without using diffusers or taking shortcuts. Our Silver Tequila was rated 93 points and we've won a number of gold medals in international competitions, typically beating out tequilas that are twice our retail price. Our customers may first sample Sparkle Donkey because of the irreverent branding, but then they become fans because of the great taste and quality."

Products:

Vodka

- Bakon Vodka—a superior quality potato vodka with a savory bacon flavor; clean, crisp, delicious, and perfect for Bloody Marys

Tequila

- Sparkle Donkey Tequila Silver—high sugar Blue Weber agave, traditional brick oven roasting, and pure volcanic spring water

Bourbon

- You're Going on a Hike—wheated bourbon, aged one year in new oak, finished with charred cherry and apple wood

- Through the Woods—straight bourbon, aged two years in new oak, finished in charred pear and peach wood

- Under the Stars—American rye, aged three years in new oak, finished in charred cherry and peach wood

DEMITRI'S BLOODY MARY MIX
SEATTLE, WASHINGTON

DEMITRI PALLIS IS A SEATTLE NATIVE, growing up in Rainier Beach. He invites me into the upstairs office of his warehouse in Georgetown, where a drum kit takes up most of the back corner. The first thing I want to know is what it was like growing up in Seattle in the 1980s.

"Pioneer Square was fun," he smiles. "It was joint cover night—you would pay the bouncer in joints for the cover charge and you would get into all the bars. This is before Belltown, before Ballard, even before Capitol Hill really popped. Between the clientele and the substances that were rolling around at the time, Pioneer Square was a hot mess."

"That sounds pretty rad," I say.

"Oh yea—it was fun," he chuckles.

In 1983 he started his career at Jake O'Shaughnessy's, a bar and restaurant in the Queen Anne neighborhood that boasted the Guiness World Record for Largest Collection of Spirits. "It wasn't fancy back then," he explains. "Every now and then you would get someone to make you a nice cocktail—a Ramos Fizz, Tequila Sunrise, Mai Tai, or Slippery Nipple—not like now." He worked there for several years, crediting the training he received for his passion and success today. "I loved making nice drinks he explains. "Every now and then you would get someone to make you a nice cocktail—a Ramos Fizz, Tequila Sunrise, Mai Tai, or Slippery Nipple—not like now." He worked there for several years, crediting the training he received for his passion and success today. "I loved making nice drinks and doing it well. I loved getting my eyeball measurements, my eyeball pours—when I'm done shaking it's to the drop, right where it's supposed to be. I really like making complicated drinks."

He left Jake's in 1986 to tend bar at The New Orleans Creole Cafe, which had a slightly different training policy than he was accustomed to. "It was a rolling trainwreck at all times," he says with a smile. "My first day, the owner tossed me the keys and said 'If you have a problem, you deal with it.'" He found the lack of standards frustrating, but does admit that it was liberating to have the freedom to do whatever he wanted. "Everyone was ordering drinks differently. They called drinks by different names. They wanted me to make drinks differently for them. I said, 'No! The drink is made this way.' I told the owner, 'Hey, at the next meeting, I have some ideas about how we can shape up and streamline everything.'"

"We don't have meetings," the owner responded. "They just cause problems."

It was during his time at the New Orleans that he was confronted with the problem he would dedicate the rest of his life to solving: making the perfect Bloody Mary mix, and making enough of it before a bar shift. "I said to myself, 'this is a nightmare. This one drink is the death of me.' If I made too much, it would spoil. If I didn't make enough, we would run out before a Seahawks game. I would go from selling $7 Bloody Marys to $2 longnecks and it just crushed my ring out."

His new colleagues avoided the task, or concocted mixes that were too spicy or too boring, and the onus fell on him to make a tasty batch that would get them through a long brunch. "At the time, even now, a lot of people were unfamiliar with how to create a base like that," he explains. "I fiddled with the recipe for about a year, so the ratio would come out tasting right. Pretty soon, the guys at The Central and Merchant's Cafe and those places said, 'Hey, mix me some of that shit, I hate making Bloody Marys!'"

"I thought, you know what? I'm going to call some people."

He brought a sample to his uncle who owned a bar in the nearby South Lake Union neighborhood, and the feedback was positive. Customers loved it, his uncle reported, and bartenders did, too, as it was simple to make. "This really makes sense!" his uncle exclaimed in his Greek accent. Demitri, aware that he was on to something, got to work. "I lived above Romeo's Pizza on Interbay for about five years. My first palette of plastic bottles showed up and the trucker was laughing at me. I had to hand carry a hundred and something cases up my stairs. My roommate was a little miffed when he came home."

Seattleites are famous for starting successful businesses in their garages; Demitri launched his empire from his apartment, punching in for long bar shifts at The New Orleans and then coming home to work on his new project until sunrise. His mixes—that today sell in bars and restaurants in all 50 states—have a humble beginning. "I remember working until three or four in the morning all the time. Hand delivering. I'd put all the stuff in my powder-white 1966 Chrysler Valiant. Someone had broken off my antenna to make a crack pipe, so I had a coat hanger on there. I've had spills, GIANT spills, in my apartment. I had a 55-gallon drum and I'd mix the stuff with a Craftsman drill."

Dry Fly Distilling

Spokane, Washington

Don Poffenroth created Dry Fly in 2007, born of two passions: his love of craft spirits, and his adoration for the Pacific Northwest. Their farm-to-bottle approach means that all ingredients are hyperlocal: all grains are sourced from family farms within 30 miles of their distillery, bar, and bottle shop location in downtown Spokane near the river. Wisota Farms supplies their wheat, barley and oats come from Danaher Farms, and the Spokane Hutterian Brethren commune provides their corn. This "grain to glass" operation is a must-visit in Eastern Washington—the state's first distillery since Prohibition.

At their downtown spot, guests can sip on their gins, vodkas, whiskeys, and bourbons via tasting flights or on the rocks. They offer a full bar, a cocktail program that highlights their award-winning products, and their line of canned cocktails. Just like their booze, the restaurant sources fresh, local ingredients for their menu. They use an in-house smoker, pita oven, and tandoor oven to whip up entrees like their smoked rainbow trout dip, tandoori chicken salad, burgers, and pulled-pork sandwiches. They also offer stewed mussels and steamed clams, flavored with the botanicals from their house gin.

Products:

- Washington Wheat Vodka—creamy, buttery, and incredibly smooth, made with locally sourced wheat (Dry Fly's first ever distilled product. This 2009 Double Gold, Best in Show at the World Spirits Competition has been a must-have for any vodka lover.)

- Washington Dry Gin—a truly unique and wonderful botanical blend of juniper, apple, coriander, mint, hops, and lavender, giving this spirit its defining Pacific Northwest feel and characteristics; light and mellow, enjoyed by non-gin lovers and gin lovers alike

- Straight Bourbon 101—the first legal bourbon made in Washington State; features corn grown by our local Hutterian settlement and triticale grown by Mitch the farmer; aged in 53-gallon American oak barrels for a minimum of three years

- Huckleberry Vodka—a soft, creamy-textured vodka made with 100 percent soft white winter wheat, a delicious wild huckleberry syrup, and an all-natural huckleberry flavoring to give it a bold flavor and bright color; bottled at a full 80 proof for superior cocktails

- Straight Washington Wheat Whiskey—The first whiskey that Dry Fly ever created, from 100 percent wheat mash bill and made completely from local grains

- Barrel Reserve Gin—Dry Fly's award-winning Washington Dry Gin, barrel-aged for a year in a used wheat whiskey barrel; not quite gin, not quite whiskey, 100 percent fantastic

Canned Cocktail Series

- Huckleberry Lemonade
- Wild Berry Hibiscus Cosmo
- Whiskey Smash
- Moscow Mule
- Spicy Lemonde
- Spiced Cranberry
- Grey-Hound
- Gin and Tonic

Unicorn Distillery

Seattle, Washington

America's first color-changing vodka and tequila were created, like all great things, in a Seattle garage. Rick and Alaina Hewitt craft small batches of their Unicorn spirits by infusing them with butterfly pea flower, which reacts to acidity by transitioning from a dark purple to a vibrant pink—perfect for wowing bar patrons. Rick hails from a brewing background, choosing the Emerald City for the location of the distillery because of the city's renowned water from the Cedar River Watershed, fed by the melting snowpack of the Cascade Range and percolated through volcanic rock. Their corn-based vodka is filtered through activated carbon then flavored with rose hips and tangerine peels, yielding a soft floral aroma and smooth finish. Their agave tequila is distilled in Alambic Armagnacais—an ancient process utilizing a special type of continuous pot still—producing a bold and balanced flavor. Both spirits have collected multiple accolades since their launch in 2021.

BEER

Alliteration Ales

Lost Grove Brewing

Barbarian Brewing

Sockeye Brewing

Bear Island Brewing Co.

Chalice Brewing

Citizen 33 Brewery

High Society Brewing

Idawild Brewing Company

Lone Mountain Farms & Brewery

Off the Rails Brewing

Star Route Brewery

WINE

Par Terre Winery

Hat Ranch Winery

Telaya Wine Co.

Split Rail Winery

Cinder Wines

Clearwater Canyon Cellars

Huston Vineyards

Rivaura Estate Vineyard and Winery

IDAHO

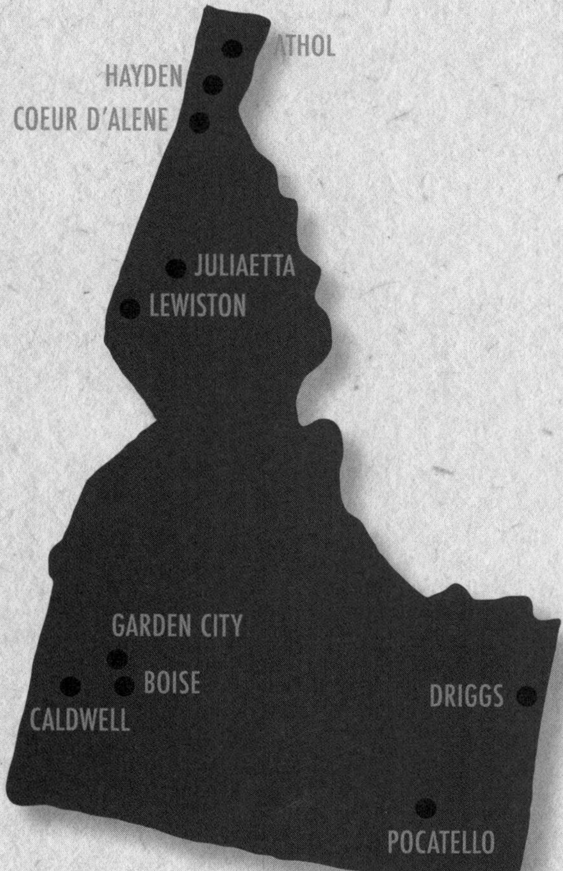

ATHOL

HAYDEN

COEUR D'ALENE

JULIAETTA

LEWISTON

GARDEN CITY

BOISE

CALDWELL

DRIGGS

POCATELLO

IDAHO

NOT UNDISCOVERED but overlooked: this is the story of The Gem State. As alcohol artisans flee the high cost of living on the coast, they descend on Boise and Coeur d'Alene to post up and activate their passions, crafting unique and flavorsome wines, beers, and spirits. Idaho has arrived, and it's time you happened upon the magical potions they are crafting.

IDAHO
BEER

———

Idaho's first brewery was opened in the 1860s, a watering hole for thirsty miners pursuing their share of the Gold Rush. Most workers were German immigrants, who arrived with pickaxes, shovels, and an insatiable love of lager. In those times, beer was quite perishable, necessitating that beer producers set up shop nomadically - as the miners moved on to the next area, so did the brewers.

Soon, the larger producers in the east would perfect pasteurization, allowing their products to be shipped nationally via rail. Idaho brewers, sensing threat,

launched a marketing campaign extolling the virtues of hyperlocal production. The outside competition proved fierce, as their products could be transported anywhere with a train station. "You're making 600 barrels a year and you're trying to compete with a guy who's making 600,000," explains historian Herman Ronnenberg. The imminent passing of Prohibition would prove fatal, as Idaho went dry in 1916. It was "the great knockout punch for American brewing," notes Ronnenberg.

For the next five or six decades, the large industrial outfits like Schlitz and Busch used their amassed capital and expertise to dominate production, capturing approximately 90 percent of the market share. It was the craft beer renaissance of the 1980s that generated the relative explosion of the Idaho brewing industry seen today. Enjoying the first Idaho Brewers Festival in 2011, journalist Guy Hand remarked "Ronnenberg was right. Looking at 1960, when not even one local brewery existed, to now, when there are enough of them crafting beer to warrant a celebration, that is magical."

Alliteration Ales

Boise, Idaho

 "Beer is half art and half science," Adam Fleck says as he shows me his garage brewery in Boise, ID. He and his partner, Shelley, founded Alliteration Ales nanobrewery with the goal of creating a "Beervana" for their customers. Adam was a homebrew hobbyist working in the semiconductor industry in Portland, Oregon, before learning the trade as a quality control chemist for craft breweries and launching his own project. "My job is to make good beer," he tells me, "and Shelley's job is to make our beer look good."

We discussed Boise and what drew them to the area to create Alliteration, the state's only licensed homebrewery. "Idaho is now worth what it should be; it's like what Portland was 20 years ago—in a good way," he tells me. However, the city's water is too low-quality for making beer, and requires a lot of filtering before use in his Pacific Northwest brewing style. They started it all with Preemptive Pale Ale, their first and flagship product. "It's hard to make great beer twice," he explains, "and you can hide anything with hops." He pours me a snifter of their American Kolsch, light, crisp and tasty. The couple feels embraced by the local beer community, invited to participate in the city's annual Shade City Brewfest.

Alliteration does not operate a brick and mortar establishment, so check their website's tap map to see what bars are pouring their brews; you may get to see Adam playing guitar in his band Whiskey Flats.

Products:

- Preemptive Pale Ale—clean, fresh, citrus
- Two-Tailed T Test Unfiltered Lager—light malt notes and smooth finish
- Borealis Baltic Porter—rich chocolate and molasses notes
- Flight of Fancy IPA— bitter citrus and fruity hops

Lost Grove Brewing

Boise, Idaho

The Greenbelt in Boise is enjoying a surge in popularity of late, and Lost Grove brewing serves up the perfect combination of brews, pizza, and live music. Jake Black launched the taproom in 2017 with a mission to provide a space for gathering and community involvement over tasty beer. They welcome families and dogs for bingo, trivia, concerts, and charity events like their Powerful Pints night, when they donate half of all sales to a local nonprofit chosen by their employees. Their mission proudly states that "Lost Grove Brewing strives for sustainable practices that help the environment through sourcing locally and reducing waste; socially responsible efforts that positively impact our communities through connection and support; and brewing recipes that create really great beer to tie it all together." As they say, "We work tirelessly to join these components to help us leave the right footprint as we seek our own lost groves."

Marketing Director Haley Robinson bought me a tasting flight and delicious Pizza-of-the-Day as we sat down to discuss their commitment to green practices. "Lost Grove is a cool brewery," she tells me, "but I'm biased of course. We are the only brewery in Idaho that has a B Corp Certification—a commitment for-profit businesses make to use their companies as a force for good in the community through increased transparency, sustainability efforts, and more." They use locally sourced ingredients and solar energy to power their efforts, and you can taste the results during the Shade City Brewfest, a celebration of beer and sustainability held at the Idaho Botanical Garden. They also donate spent grain to local animal farms—a near-universal practice in Tree City—and purchase carbon offsets for their ClimateHound certification.

Haley's pride was most prevalent, however, when we discussed their beers. They just began the second year of their barrel-aged series, for which they hire a local artist-in-residence to design the labels for five new creations annually. We sipped their Yersinia Imperial Stout with a cool blue label from artist Miguel Almeida on the bottle. Their rotating line of hazy IPAs are spotlighted in the

Robot Series, named after things that would be "super scary if they turned into robots" such as Robot Grizzly and Robot Dentist. Seasonal experimentals abound on tap, but must-try flagship products include the Margot Amber ("She's the girl you can take home to Mom one weekend, but she'll break into your house and steal your golf clubs the next.") and Teddy Bear Picnic Golden Session Ale ("Kids need a favorite teddy bear; you need a favorite everyday beer.").

Products:

- Teeny Tiny Cowboy Everyday Beer—light, refreshing, and easy to drink
- First Sight IPA— juicy hops and balanced bitterness
- Ghost Town Coffee Hazelnut Porter—dark nuttiness and smooth finish
- Margot Amber—beautiful color and caramel malt
- Acid Raindrops Series Kettle Sours

Barbarian Brewing

Boise, Idaho

 Standing in Barbarian's Garden City Taproom—their second location—becomes all the more impressive once founder James "The Barbarian" Long tells me that it all began in a strip mall just seven years earlier. He was a nurse in California, and met his future wife and partner Bre on a blind date. (She was actually there to meet James's roommate, not him.) They started homebrewing after a Belgian nurse introduced them to traditional lambics and sours, and soon realized that it was time to launch an enterprise. "Every closet in the house was filled with barrels," James tells me.

"Why the f**k not?" is the official motto of Barbarian (named for their dog, Conan), as the tap list is as filled with German-style pilsners and lagers as it is seasonal experimentals, like their brewed Thai Iced Tea Ice Cream Ale. Their 90 oak barrels hold bourbon stouts, hazy and West Coast IPAs, and their full program of sours. It all began with their Little Wolf IPA flavored with Citra, Mosaic, and El Dorado hops, and their Belgian-style tripel. They are the only brewery in Idaho to use cool ship technique, wherein the wort is cooled in an open-top vessel and airborne yeasts and bacteria inoculate the beer naturally in spontaneous fermentation.

Barbarian has two locations: their brewing taproom in Garden City, and their Downtown Beer Bar. Most of what they make is only available on tap, though you can purchase canned products to take home. The Taproom is a large and inviting space with high ceilings. They welcome both children and dogs inside and on the expansive patio. A rotating array of food trucks feed hungry visitors, as live music plays on. The Downtown Beer Bar does not allow minors, but the grown-ups can munch on street tacos and breakfast burritos from Calle 75. Mocktails are always available at both locations.

Products:

- Lush IPA—West Coast style with tropical hops

- Waffle Cone Stout—aged in bourbon oak barrels

- Hard seltzers—Wolf Paw—with real passion fruit, guava, and agave nectar

- Fruited sours—kettle-style and German-style goses

Sockeye Brewing

Boise, Idaho

"Sockeye has endeared itself to the city," explains Director of Marketing Tyson Cardon as he shows me around their expansive new downtown Alehouse. "We are a destination for Boise." Launched in a garage in 1996, Sockeye has since earned just about every superlative imaginable - they are Idaho's top-selling brewery and most-awarded craft brewery. Their flagship ale, Dagger Falls IPA, is the state's most popular craft beer, as evidenced when we walk through the bar and have to search for an open table at 5 p.m. on a Thursday. "This is actually just the soft opening, we're not technically open yet," Tyson beams. "We're in a good spot." Their ribbon-cutting was scheduled the following week.

Their 12,000-foot Alehouse is a destination, indeed. It features 4,000 square feet of patio space adjacent to their nine-hole putting course. Family and dog-friendly, they serve up elevated pub fare (try the classic Alehouse burger) alongside their year-round and seasonal drafts, craft cocktails, non-alcoholic options (like their Hop Water), and guest ciders. The building is LEED-certified for energy efficiency. They implement a wastewater treatment program ("we have to take care of the river," notes Tyson) and donate their spent grain to local ani-

mal farms. Ninety-six percent of all ingredients used in production are sourced from the Pacific Northwest. The brand-new space is the perfect spot to post up after a Broncos game, to enjoy a sampling flight, and to catch every sporting event on their myriad televisions.

Sockeye features a series of year-round brews, as well as seasonals, experimentals, and barrel-aged batches. Guests can check their website to see what's on tap, or just show up and ask the bartender what they are serving up that day. "We value innovation," Tyson says. "We are a legacy brewery with an eye to the future."

Products:

Year-Round Series

- Powerhouse Porter—the award-winningest beer in Idaho
- Dagger Falls IPA—citrus, pine, and more awards
- Lonesome Larry Lager—golden Munich-style helles
- Angel's Perch Amber—toasted, sweet malt

Seasonals

- Socktoberfest Lager —rich, smooth, German malted barley
- Starlight Honey Steam Beer —springtime ale with Star Thistle honey
- Winterfest Strong Ale—toffee, caramel, barley
- Una Mas Cerveza Con Lima—Mexican lager with a hint of lime

Bear Island Brewing Co.

Boise, Idaho

The origins of Bear Island are best told in their words:

Once Upon a time in Cascade, Idaho, the Westover family was enjoying time at their to-be cabin site (aka, staying in tents while building the family cabin). Being surrounded by wilderness, the children nervously asked their parents about the possibility of running into a bear. The parents told their children that when Cascade Reservoir freezes over in the winter, all of the bears go out to the island in the middle to hibernate. And when they wake up in the spring, the lake is thawed out and they are stuck out there! Therefore, there is no need to be afraid of the bears because they are all on "Bear Island."

–www.bearislandbrewing.com

Steve and Beth Bechtel are both Navy veterans, having worked in explosive ordnance disposal—great experience for those launching a business where things can blow up in your face at any time. In fact, every employee of Bear Island is either a military veteran or married to one. "Proud to have served our country, and now our community" is the proud motto of "Boise's Biggest Little Brewery." They homebrewed in their garage for the first five years (now the home of Alliteration Ales), and expanded to occupy the renovated Firehouse #6 downtown, where guests can bring their dogs and kids and enjoy pints of their year-round "Foundational" series, seasonal experimentals, and guest ciders.

Products:

- Idaho Potato Ale—IPA with russet potatoes and specialty hops

- Brewhouse #6—Euro-style pilsner named for their firehouse taproom

- Prime in Ale—traditional American pale with notes of lemon and grapefruit

- Ammo Bocks—German dunkles bock style, caramel and toffee flavors

Chalice Brewing

Coeur d'Alene, Idaho

*Chalice Brewing was founded to elevate the craft beer industry through contin-
uous innovation, influenced by the community for the community. Community
is the core of Chalice Brewing and is embedded into the fabric of the brewery.
Ingredients for the line of Chalice-brewed beers, ciders, and mead will be as local-
ly-sourced as possible. The brewery is a Coeur d'Alene hub, supporting local music,
art, and food, while providing a space for gathering and connecting.*
–www.chalicebrewing.com

When choosing the spot to launch Chalice, the owners wanted to reno-
vate and preserve a part of Coeur d'Alene. They chose their location on
Sherman Avenue, a century-old building whose wallpaper, they soon discovered, was obscuring a foundation of beautiful brickwork. "The original bricks
are the cornerstone of the brewery," owner Brian Engdahl says proudly. "They
weren't easy to uncover, but we're glad it was possible."

Brian, raised by entrepreneurs, wanted to launch his own brew project at an early age. He cut his chops at Widmer Brothers after obtaining his degree in Fermentation Science at Oregon State University. Later he accepted the head brewer position at Ancestry Brewing in Tualatin, Oregon, winning them multiple awards. He chose Coeur d'Alene to set his own enterprise in motion because of its sense of community and natural beauty.

Products:

- Prost Falls Dunkel—a classic Munich dunkel characterized by malty amber color and slight roastiness

- TeaSB Earl Grey ESB—a twist on the classic style, using pounds of Smith Teamaker's Lord Bergamot, Earl Grey Tea, to give this beer an amazing floral and citrusy aroma

- Sunshine Daydream Hoppy Pilsner—the second beer in the "Campfire Series" collaboration with Chalice Brewing and Trails End Brewing; a hop-forward Pilsner that is easy, crisp, and citrusy

Citizen 33 Brewery

Driggs, Idaho

Our goal is to establish a destination in the city of Driggs, Idaho. Citizen 33 was built for the community members and for visitors to Teton Valley to come together and celebrate this amazing place with delicious food and cold craft beer. Cheers to the citizens, "a native or inhabitant" of Route 33!

At Citizen 33, we look at what ingredients we have locally, and what beers we can make with them. This does limit us stylistically, and there could be beers we will never make. These sacrifices, however, allow us to make a unique and truly local beer. The "newspeak" of local brewing! What we offer is beer that is entirely Idaho. You are drinking Idaho in a glass! The base malt barley is grown and malted in the Snake River Plains west of our valley near Idaho Falls, ID. Depending on the recipe, roughly 5 percent to 30 percent of our grain bill is specialty malt from Weyermann in Bamberg, Germany, as they carry the highest quality specialty malts available. All of the hops we use are grown in western Idaho. In the pursuit to create the best beer possible, we continue to seek out the best ingredients grown in Idaho!

–Lisa Hanley, Citizen 33

Products:

- C33 Locals Lager—American-style, light, for the locals

- Idaho ObSESSION IPA—citrusy, fruity, piney

- Newspeak Mountain IPA—sweet and complex, loaded with hops

- Citizen Pub Ale—English-style, medium body, and smooth

- Blackfoot Stout—American stout with coffee and dark chocolate notes

High Society Brewing
Hayden, Idaho

"High Society Brewing was created to give the craft beer community an example of what a nanobrewery could do in the shadows of giant craft behemoths. We are super passionate about the craft beer industry, the people behind the beer, and the togetherness that we share through this golden liquid."
—R. Austin Hildebrand, Founder

 R. Austin cut his teeth in the beer industry as a wholesaler for MillerCoors, shifting his focus as of late toward creating and growing independent craft breweries (such as Hunga Dunga and Bombastic Brewing). In 2021, he launched his own enterprise, High Society Brewing in Hayden, Idaho.

"We are all on this earth for a reason," he explains. "A huge part of this life is the connection we make with others and the things we do throughout this journey. Human relationship is something unlike anything else and it should be highlighted and celebrated. That is why we are making it our mission to not only make great beer, but do great things with that beer. We want to connect with our community, supporters, customers, and everyone in between. Our mission is to create great beers, deliver an enhanced experience, and impart our own take on life. This is more than just another beer and more than just another brewery. This is what happens when you elevate your beer."

Their brewing process is on a nano scale, allowing Hildebrand to regularly try out different styles and experiment with everything. That ability to diversify and create adds a touch of uniqueness that many medium-large scale breweries cannot achieve. They even use ingredients from their own family farm. "My mother-in-law owns a farm in Garwood, Idaho. We utilize wildflower honey, raspberries, dried lavender, pumpkin puree, toasted pumpkin, and wild hops from there when possible. We also have been known to gather local North Idaho ingredients to use in our beers, like fresh wild huckleberry."

Their beers are available on draft and occasionally in the bottle/can. They self-distribute to a small number of taphouses, restaurants, and bars within the local area. Their taphouse offers a pub food menu and is kid and dog friendly. They have an outside patio area in the front of the brewery that allows customers to relax and enjoy a view of Canfield Mountain.

Products:

- Anarchy Amber—lightly malted and subtly sweet American amber ale with just the right amount of Perle hops added

- River Sipper Kölsch—this flagship kölsch is the closest thing you'll get to a traditional German kölsch in North Idaho; they also make variants of this, such as White Peach Kölsch and Wildflower Honey Kölsch

- Garwood Honey Brown Ale—an ode to their family farm, highlighting all-natural wildflower honey from the farm

- London Nights Lavender Stout—another ode to the family farm, using a lengthy grain bill accompanied by two unique hops, Madagascar vanilla beans (both regular and bourbon soaked), an English ale yeast, a touch of lactose, and the finishing touch of dried lavender heads

- Revolution Porter—showcases caramel, chocolate, and dark malts that pair perfectly with the Chinook/Willamette hops

- Too Eazy West Coast IPA—named in honor of one of the owner's favorite rap artists of today (G Eazy), showcasing the infamous Centennial hop and including a generous dry hop addition

- Liberty Pale Ale—a smooth, slightly hoppy, and easy-drinking pale for anytime of year

- Seditious Juicy IPA—showcases a delicious Idaho pilsner malt, a touch of a special malt, and then adds heaps of Strata hops to make a juice bomb

- IRA AF Dry Irish Stout—this beer is only released once a year and has been demanded (almost violently) to be a monthly staple at the taproom; crafted from multiple types of barley and an Irish ale yeast to create a smooth drinking dark stout with a hint of dryness on the finish

Idawild Brewing Company

Garden City, Idaho

Matt and Cortni Nader are longtime Idaho residents with a passion for great beer and the outdoors. What began as a homebrew hobby in their spare bedroom has blossomed into a five-barrel production facility and taproom in Garden City, near Boise. Matt is the brewmaster, combining traditional techniques with modern creativity. Cortni is the designer, forming the taproom to offer a welcoming atmosphere for guests to enjoy delicious craft beer with the people they love.

We specialize in thoughtfully crafted small-batch brews to satisfy both the adventurous beer drinker and those who tend to stick to conventional styles. Our specialties are smooth yet flavorful hazy IPAs and crisp, easy-drinking kettle sours. We offer options that you can't find anywhere else, and the ever-growing tap list is sure to have a perfect option for everyone in your crew!

Their taproom has outdoor patio seating, bar stools, couches, and tables for any type of group. There is also a large game room with billiards, shuffleboard, arcade games, and darts. Little ones and barky bois are always invited.

Products:

- A Kölsch with No Name—a traditional light, refreshing, German-style brew
- Blackberry Lime Sour—kettle sour finished with 176 pounds of blackberry and 44 pounds of lime
- Boiseberry Milkshake IPA—hazy IPA brewed with Simcoe hops and milk sugar, finished with blackberry and raspberry
- El Fiero Hazy IPA—chili-spiced mango hazy IPA finished with 220 pounds of mango and four pounds of serrano peppers
- Fireside S'Mores Stout—oatmeal stout brewed with 20 pounds of graham crackers, milk sugar, and vanilla beans

- First Light DDH Hazy IPA—double dry-hopped with 100 percent galaxy hops

- Kaldi's Curiosity Coffee Stout—full-bodied stout finished with a Café Mulé nitro cold brew

- Motherlode Golden Ale—it's a golden ale

- Oktoberfest Märzen Lager—a traditional Oktoberfest-style German lager with a toasty, clean, and dry finish

- Cobble Cobble Sour—kettle sour brewed with cinnamon and nutmeg and finished with 176 pounds of peaches

- Pumpkin Ale—amber ale brewed with pumpkin, cinnamon, nutmeg, cloves, and ginger, then finished with Tahitian vanilla beans

- Willie's West Coast IPA—brewed with Cashmere, Centennial, Amarillo, Azacca, and Citra hops

- Spiced Wassail Sour—kettle sour finished with tart green apple, cranberry, orange peel, cinnamon, and clove

Lone Mountain Farms & Brewery

Athol, Idaho

Farm craft beer is the passion of Luke and Emily Black, a husband-and-wife duo obsessed with growing fields of flavor. The outcome is Lone Mountain Farms, a small, diverse operation in Athol, Idaho. Here you'll find hops, rare grains, and produce alongside flocks of chickens scavenging for treats. Their proximity to the Selkirk Mountains allows for just the right amount of moisture from autumn to spring, with a warm and dry summer. The taste of the farm's terroir truly shines through their craftsmanship. Luke is the grain farmer and head cook, his calling in the fields and kitchen. Emily is the hop and produce farmer and marketing director, happy amongst her veggies and sharing their story. "The hops spring forth like asparagus shoots in early spring and climb their way up to the sky until late summer harvest," they say. "And we grow over ten varieties to give diversity to our beer bittering and aroma."

FARM-CRAFT BEER

NET CONTENTS
1 PINT
16 FL. OZ.

Off the Rails Brewing

Pocatello, Idaho

At Off the Rails, we strive to have a kick-ass environment with great food and great beer. Everything you see in Off the Rails is tailored to fit our story. We want you to enjoy our handcrafted beer and delicious food all in a custom-designed and unique environment. Our tables and chairs are specially made from rebar, train wood, and train fabric. We branded every table with a railroad spike and a few tables have actual railroad spikes inserted in the center. Our stunning bar top was made by a local company in Boise. We want everything in our brewery to feel like an entirely new experience, every time. Everything in Off the Rails represents our story. We represent the history of old town Pocatello and the foundation this city was built on. The foundation that revolves around supporting local and keeping our history alive. We strive to be as historic and unforgettable as the railroads of Pocatello. We invite all of you to become part of our story. . . There's plenty of room, so all aboard, we're heading Off the Rails!

Products:

- Feeley Irish Red—light, dry, biscuit, caramel, toffee
- Smooth Hoperator Mango Hazy—New England hazy pale ale bursting with mango and citrus aroma right off the nose

Star Route Brewery

Pocatello, Idaho

 Star Route—named for the former Louisiana address of the founder— was born of passion for the microbrewery revolution. Chris White spent a decade traveling for business, always sampling the local beers along the way. It was Colorado's booming brewing community that inspired him to start homebrewing: "I drank as much as I could, and I gave the rest away," he jokingly recalls. The pandemic loomed over the launch of his Pocatello brewery, but it is now up and running with his proprietary brews, named after his friends, family, and special places he has visited. Patrons can savor homemade pizzas and salads and daily drink specials.

Products:

- Offerle Hefe

- Brain Fog Hazy IPA

- Dark Knite Oatmeal Stout

- Backstrap Black IPA

IDAHO
WINE

—

In Idaho, we are the oft-forgotten "other" state in the Pacific Northwest. Which is rather ironic, considering that the first wineries in the Pacific Northwest were located in Idaho, and that Idaho had a nationally renowned wine industry until Prohibition.
–John H. Thorngate, Ph.D., Applications Chemist, Research & Development, Constellation Wines U.S.

Idaho's first grapes—royal muscadine—were planted in 1864 in Lewiston. Falling victim to the Pacific Northwest temperance movement like their neighbors to the west, Idaho voted for Prohibition years before the federal law was implemented—and grapes would not be planted again until 1970. Gregory Eaves opened the first winery after Prohibition's repeal in 1935. It would be *37 years* until the second—Chateau Juliaette—was bonded.

Southern Idaho—home of the Snake River Valley AVA, established in 2007 and covering 8,000 square miles—features ideal growing conditions for wine grapes. The cold winters stave off disease and pests, while causing the vines to go dormant and save up their carbohydrates. The pairing of warm days with cool nights fosters a favorable balance of acids and sugars. The relative lack of rainfall prevents woes experienced by their wetter colleagues in Oregon such as mold, rot, and dilution of sugars by early rainfall.

Idaho's wine industry—nascent by PNW standards—is on the cusp of a boom. In 1999, there were 656 acres of vineyards in the state, and that area has tripled in size since. There are now three AVAs in the state (Snake River as the largest, plus the Lewis-Clark AVA and Eagle Foothills sub-AVA). There is also a unique emergent "urban region" in Boise, as winemakers are growing fruit and producing their own wines right in the city.

Par Terre Winery

Garden City, Idaho

"There is no perfection in dance," Travis Walker explains to me. "You are always learning. You get used to rejection and used to failure." Ballet is how Travis met his wife, Mallory, both accomplished professional dancers from northern California. Their field brutal and unforgiving, the couple aged out in their thirties and relocated to Boise, Idaho, to begin their second act: winemaking. Travis had been teaching himself the craft in their home garage, and enrolled in Walla Walla Community College's Enology and Viticulture program to earn his degree. Mallory herself completed a business degree. Just as the pair had danced together before, they were now ready for a new pas de deux making booze. They began producing wine from local grapes in 2016, naming their venture Par Terre, a dance term meaning "on the ground."

As I walked into their tasting room in Garden City, I was greeted by Travis and their friendly brown dog, Roux. The large space is part winery, part dance hall, serving as headquarters for their Project Flux dance program directed by Lydia Sakolsky-Basquill. Guests can grab a glass or bottle and watch dancers create and choreograph movement to their selections. They conduct dance classes, oyster pairings, and painting nights here. Encore Club members also enjoy members-only events. Bring your dog and have a tasting flight of their unique creations, including cabernet franc, viognier, and merlots from the Snake River Valley AVA.

Products:

- 2020 Merlot—plush tannins, red fruit, violet, and hint of vanilla
- 2020 Cabernet Sauvignon—aged in French oak with notes of dried herbs, currant, and plum
- 2020 Cabernet Franc—bold raspberry and black pepper
- 2021 Viognier—apricot nectar, honeysuckle, and rosé
- 2021 En L'air Rosé—crisp blend of syrah, merlot, and cab sauv grapes

HAT RANCH
WINERY

Hat Ranch Winery

Caldwell, Idaho

"Drink more Idaho wine!" exclaims Erin Rutherford, the tasting room manager at Hat Ranch Winery in Caldwell, a 40-minute drive west from Boise. Established in 2011, they took their name from the Wyoming settlement of founder Tim Harless's great-grandparents. The accolades arrived immediately, as their first vintages of chardonnay and riesling won gold and silver medals, respectively. By the end of the decade, they had won Idaho Winery of the Year (2019), after surviving the great Snowpocalypse during the winter of 2016 that dropped three feet of snow on the region. ("It took us years to recover from that," Erin tells me.)

Tim is a graduate of Grayson College, studying viticulture and enology. He also earned a degree in aerospace engineering, and incorporates his technical knowledge and eye for detail into his winemaking. He chose the Sunnyslope Wine Trail in the Snake River AVA for its terroir, microclimate, and close community. In 2014, they purchased the neighboring estate of Vale, and you can sample and purchase from both wineries at their tasting room. Winemaker Will Wetmore sources local grapes (in addition to their own) and uses conventional practices to produce about 3,000 cases per year.

Products:

- 2020 Hat Trick Red—rotating blend of three grapes that changes every year
- 2021 Dry Moscato—winner of Best of Show in *Wall Street Journal*
- Muscat Ottonel—a spicy delight
- 2020 Cabernet Franc—bold and superb

Telaya Wine Co.

Garden City, Idaho

A recurring story in my journey across the PNW is the tale of duos leaving their lucrative careers to start new chapters in life producing booze, and Telaya founders Earl and Carrie Sullivan are a stellar example. Earl was a traveling pharmaceutical executive, spending 280 days per year on the road; Carrie was an accomplished veterinarian. "We wanted to create a project in which we could work together as a family and instill core values in our children," Earl explains as we chat at their tasting room on a snowy afternoon. "We wanted to do something that was intellectually stimulating and that would instill a work ethic in our kids, and I wanted to work with my hands." He walked away from the C-suite to become a "cellar rat" and learn from other winemakers. They started creating wine using Washington grapes in 2008 in a workspace they shared with two other wineries; now, they crank out over 200 tons per year as one of Idaho's largest producers.

Telaya (the name is a combination of Tetons and La Playa, Earl and Carrie's two favorite places to visit) was conceived as "an oasis of comfort and welcoming to learn about wine," Earl explains. They operate the winery with a "high touch" service model, focusing on hospitality and education. All employees enjoy salary and benefits, in their belief that job security correlates with excellent service. Tipping is not allowed, and they "keep the knife sharp" by inviting all employees on two annual company trips for fun and education. "If employees are doing a good job, then the trip is for fun," Earl tells me. "But if not, then the trip is for education." After the trip, the team all gets together to discuss the travel and learn from what they experienced. "Wine can be a uniter—there is a huge education component to what we do here."

The current tasting room opened in 2016 on the Boise Greenbelt alongside the river, where the city has been supporting the emergence of a "Beverage

Corridor," a high concentration of wineries and breweries. "A rising tide lifts all boats," Earl says proudly. The place was crackling with energy during a weekday afternoon, and it was quickly apparent that Telaya plays an important role in the community; they even teach blending classes in their backroom production space. The tasting room boasts a brand-new deck with fire pits and is family and dog-friendly. It also hosts a rotating series of food trucks, and guests are welcome to bring in any food they wish. The newly renovated Riverside Hotel—Idaho's second largest hotel—sits next door, and is a fantastic choice for visitors to post up and plan their travel along the Corridor.

The Sullivans operate the front of the house and wine production with an impressive focus on sustainable practices. All glass is sourced in the United States. They installed an ozone cleaning system that kills 100 percent of microbes using zero chemicals. ("If you can smell anything, it's not clean," Earl tells me.) The charcuterie snack packs they offer are packaged in 100 percent reusable containers with reusable cutlery. Lighting is produced with energy-efficient LEDs, and they are working with the city of Boise on a biofuels initiative for their compostable spent waste.

Products:

- 2021 Turas—syrah-based blend with rich color and full body

- 2021 Malbec—cherry, licorice, and blackberry notes

- 2021 Petit Verdot—leather, baking spices, and cola

- 2021 Cabernet Sauvignon—featuring grapes from two different estates in Washington State

Split Rail Winery
Garden City, Idaho

"We dig wine, we love Idaho, we grew up in a farming community and so we figured what the hell, let's make some wine [in Idaho]. That to us is a beautiful story, based on love and driven by heartache."
–An Uneducated Philosopher

"Our goal is to make the guest taste something new," Jed Glavin explains, showing me around his funky tasting room in Garden City. Jed's parents imparted upon him a fascination for wine during his youth in Twin Falls, Idaho. After learning enology and sharing equipment with a local winemaker, he and his wife, Laura, founded Split Rail Winery after years of trial and error crushing grapes in their garage. The space that used to be an auto body shop now plays synth music over the speakers and hosts tastings of their unique, experimental batches. "We never make the same wine twice," Jed says proudly.

Everything about wine production here is fun, inventive, and new-wave. Jed is aging wine in imported concrete, sandstone, and clay vessels; making vermouth from chardonnay to host cocktail nights; using carbonic fermentation to make big, unfiltered juicy blends; and adding citrus notes with acacia wood barrels. This ethos of "exploratory winemaking" as they call it produces some truly tasty products that guests won't find anywhere else; nothing is sweetened or de-acified here. They offer charcuterie, host food trucks, welcome families and dogs, and are expanding their outdoor patio. Guests can purchase their wines by the keg, the can, or, of course, glass bottles with their creative and colorful labels.

Products:

- 2021 White Noise Pét-Nat—sparkling dry riesling

- 2021 Daft Pink Brut Rosé—syrah injected with bubbles

- 2021 Exploding Mirror White—chardonnay and grenache blanc blend

- 2021 Yin & Yang White—skin-fermented tannic fruity-funk

- 2020 Vermouth—sauvignon blanc steeped with herbs, botanicals, and agave

Cinder Wines

Garden City, Idaho

Cinder Wines founder Melanie Krause grew up gardening with her family in Boise, Idaho. She and her siblings would harvest, cook, and preserve their fruits and vegetables, which instilled in her a lifelong passion for agriculture. After graduating from Washington State University, she "got her farmer's tan" working as a vineyard technician at Stimson Lane (now part of Chateau Ste. Michelle) and making her own wine at home. She worked her way to enologist at Canoe Ridge Estate, then launched her own wine consulting business in Idaho. Deciding it was time to create and activate her own brand, she began Cinder Wines (named for the volcanic cinder underneath the Snake River Vineyards) in a collaborative workspace with colleagues from Vale, Syringa, Coiled, and Telaya wineries. By 2016, she had purchased the space for her own winery and now creates delicious wines with grapes sourced only from the Snake River Valley AVA.

For their tasting room in Garden City, reservations are recommended but walk-ins are welcome. They offer guided tasting flights, charcuterie, and chocolates. Cinder Wine Club members enjoy multiple customizable cases per year, as well as members-only experience and tastings, and may rent their art gallery mezzanine for private events.

All visitors should taste their Dry Viognier, their flagship wine and the reason that Melanie created Cinder:

"Viognier is the grape that brought me back to Idaho and it continues to be central to our love affair with the Snake River Valley. I often describe this wine as the red wine drinker's white wine because of its powerful flavors and considerable mouthfeel. A great viognier should have aromas to seduce your nose and a body that makes you glad to be alive. Enjoy the Queen of the White Wines in the Snake River Valley."

As well as their 2020 Tempranillo:

There are a few classic grape varieties in the world that demand specific conditions to thrive. One of those grapes is Tempranillo. Soon after our Idaho journey started, we found out how well-suited it is to our hot, dry, high-elevation vineyards of the Snake River Valley. I feel very fortunate to be able to work with this grape and uncover what it is capable of, especially in the Snake River Valley. I find Tempranillo ideal for sipping while you share life and laughter with friends. So here's to the grape that thrives in the desert and to its new American roots!

Products:

- 2022 Verdejo—rare-in-the-U.S. Spanish grape with pear blossom, vanilla, and peach notes

- 2021 Syrah—inky purple color with full-bodied aroma

- 2020 Valentina—cabernet, merlot, and malbec blend with cherry and espresso

- 2021 Rosé of Grenache—light floral notes and lively acidity

Clearwater Canyon Cellars

Lewiston, Idaho

"We look at each vintage as an opportunity to explore the wine characteristics that are unique to that year," says Coco Umiker, the founder and owner of Clearwater Canyon Cellars. Coco, along with her husband, Karl (a transplant from the Ozarks known as "The Vine Whisperer"), grows merlot, syrah, cab sauv, petit verdot, cab franc, chardonnay, viognier, riesling, muscat canelli, and orange muscat here in the Lewis-Clark Valley, on a north-facing slope overlooking the Clearwater River. Since their initial harvest of merlot in 2003, they have won both Idaho Winery of the Year (2015) and Pacific Northwest Winery of the Year (2020) from *Wine Press Northwest*.

Their origin story dates back over a century, as Coco's farm in Lewiston had been in the family for generations. After she finished studying microbiology and biochemistry at the University of Idaho, she convinced her grandfather to rent her a portion of the acreage for winemaking. Grandpa Ralph hopped on his tractor alongside Coco and Karl to plant what would become Umiker Estate Vineyard. Since wrapping up her doctorate work in the Enology and Viticulture program at Washington State University, Coco has joined Karl full-time to run Clearwater Canyon Cellars.

Coco and Karl use their own grapes in addition to fruit from farms in the Columbia Valley AVA, Horse Heaven Hills AVA, Rattlesnake Hills AVA, and the Yakima Valley.

Products:

- 2021 Renaissance Red—explosive aromas of candied cherries and plums, violets, and warm cinnamon rolls; flavors of blueberries and blackberries and a drizzle of caramel linger with round, rich tannins

- 2022 Estate Rosé of Syrah—light peachy pink with aromas of kiwi-strawberry, vanilla bean, and cherry blossoms

- 2022 Albariño—aromas of fresh grapefruit and lime zest, crystallized ginger, and a dusting of limestone; a medley of citrus and green apple flavors and juicy, lip-smacking acidity

Huston Vineyards

Caldwell, Idaho

Gregg and Mary Alger's vineyard is located in Southern Idaho's Snake River Valley AVA along the Sunnyslope Wine Trail. As farmers first, their wines begin in the vineyards, whether from their own vineyard or a neighbor in the AVA. With over 40 different lots, every site brings a unique terroir component to their wines. Their mission is simple: great wine, great foods, great friends, the best of times.

Nestled in a corner of vast farmland, the area has a long, rich agricultural history. The four distinct seasons give way in the spring to blossoming fruit orchards, vineyards, and 100 different crops. The long summer days and dry, cool nights extend into the fall season, providing the optimum harvesting bounty. The area's farming history is a century-plus success story, with sunshine in abundance, dry, arid conditions, yet with ample water for irrigation from Huston's extensive storage systems. Vineyard plantings in the area took hold in the area around 50 years ago, and the viticulture designation was established in 2007. The relatively young wine region continues to expand, with soil, climate, and elevation on par with some of the very finest wine regions worldwide.

The warm days ripen the fruit, and cool nights conserve tannins and acids—creating fruit-forward wines with complex structure. Well-draining, rich, volcanic soil and ample water are both key to superb conditions. There you will find the collaboration of dedicated growers and passionate winemakers. They are immersed in the ancient, fascinating process of growing fruit, from bud break to a fermented pour—and they love sharing it with visitors. Huston Vineyards is the perfect entry point to the Sunnyslope Wine Trail. Enjoy their wines in an

unpretentious farm setting that is as inviting as the expansive shade of their towering locust tree.

As Huston's proprietors, Gregg and Mary are meticulous in every way, their fingerprints on everything from pruning shears to clone selections, from racking, barreling, and bottling to supervising the entire operation.

Their passion is shared in the welcoming winery, located near their farmhouse adjacent to the vineyards. This platform allows them to showcase the beauty of bringing local produce, fruit, and proteins grown in the region, paired with the perfect world-class wine.

Huston Vineyards is on Chicken Dinner Road, which has its own history behind its unique name. Legend has it that an Idaho Governor was persuaded to fix the old country road by way of a delicious chicken dinner. The farm cook served up a fine feast, and the sign directing the governor to the dinner remained long after the deal was struck. You could say this very same determination and gastronomical excellence is carried on by the area's modern day vintners. Their line of table wines, Chicken Dinner Red and Chicken Dinner White, are award-winning wine blends, proudly offered at their tasting barn.

Products:

- 2021 Malbec—rich blackberry colors and aromas of dried blueberries and allspice, displaying flavors of plum and black currant with supple tannins and a spicy yet lingering finish

- 2022 Dry Riesling—light lime in color with aromas of apricot and peach, as well as stone fruit flavors with lively acidity

- 2020 Merlot—a deep ruby red color with aromas of smoky bacon and black cherry with flavors of cedar and vanilla that are sure to please the most particular palate

- 2020 Cabernet Sauvignon—rich dark berry color and aromas of currant and black cherry with dark fruit and earthy flavors

- 2020 Petite Syrah/Cabernet Sauvignon Blend—bursting with aromas of fruit, black currant, and blueberry from the Petite Sirah, with black cherry notes from the Cabernet. Vanilla, black pepper, and some spicy, herbal hints round out the nose

- 2020 Syrah—aromas of earth and violets and flavors of blackberry and espresso, with a velvety texture balanced against a peppery finish

Rivaura Estate Vineyard and Winery

Juliaetta, Idaho

The Rivaura vineyards are ideally situated to grow grapes to make superb wines. The elevation, soils, and climate are identical to some of the best vineyards in the Walla Walla Valley. I believe that some of the finest wines ever produced from Idaho grapes will be sourced from these vineyards.
–Dr. Kevin Pogue, VinTerra Consulting

The Hewett family have been homesteaders in the Lewis-Clark Valley for over a century, cultivating a close working relationship with and reverence for the land they call home on the Clearwater River. Rivaura, planted in 2014, is "the latest manifestation of the Hewetts' determination to do everything to a high standard in a humble, fiercely devoted way." Ron Hewett Sr. is the patriarch of the clan, with Ron Jr., Jane, Reece, Shannon, and their sons Lane and Vince playing their respective roles in growing and production in tandem with Winemaker Billo Naravane. They have taprooms both here in Juliaetta

and their latest enterprise in Coeur D'Alene, where guests can enjoy flights, private winemaker tastings, and beers on tap.

Grapes: cabernet franc, cabernet sauvignon, grenache, malbec, merlot, petit verdot, syrah, and viognier

Products:

- 2019 River Ranch Red—deep ruby-purple color with lovely bouquet of cassis, black cherry, dried herbs, tobacco, and damp earth; very well balanced with refreshing acidity and supple tannins

- 2019 Merlot—palate notes of black cherry, black plum, licorice, cigar tobacco, gravel, and dark chocolate with nuances of nutmeg and cardamom; a long finish echoing notes of black plum, dried thyme, and dark chocolate

Clint Hoiland

—

TWISTED VINE WINE TOURS
LEWISTON, IDAHO

Where are you from?

The Hoiland family homestead is in northern Idaho, east of Coeur d'Alene, where my great-grandfather emigrated from Norway. It remains within the family. My father got a job as a teacher in Kamiah, in the heart of the Nez Perce Reservation, when I was in the fifth grade, and I have a great love for northern Idaho.

What's your professional/educational background?

I have my bachelor of science in psychology from the University of Idaho.

When did you launch Twisted Vine?

In 2016.

What inspired you to start a wine tour business?

Everyone was always amazed at how great local wines were. Local wineries were winning gold medals and best of class at prestigious national and international wine competitions. However, the many visitors who came to experience the myriad of outdoor recreational activities in our region often left without even knowing there were wineries here. It became my mission to change that.

What motivates you to introduce people to Idaho wine?

The grapes that are grown in the Lewis-Clark Valley have a history of excellence since the first commercial vineyard was planted in 1872. The wines that are produced from them make the natural grandeur of our area so much more special. From the call of a hawk on the wing, overlooking the steep hillsides covered in natural grasses and small shrubs that plunge over 2,000 feet to the quiet confluence of the Clearwater and Snake rivers, to the sound of laughter in town and having people greet you, or at least nod and smile as you walk past, this rural life is best enjoyed with wine. And if they are from outside the area, I want them to open that bottle when they get home, and share with their friends stories of the incredible sights and friendly people they encountered.

How does it make you feel when your visitor clients enjoy and learn about Idaho wine for the first time?

I love watching the expression on my guests' faces (more especially when they are from California) as they cautiously take that first sip. . .and are delighted to be surprised. It is a mark of distinction how hard our wine-makers work to ensure quality, and it shows in every sip.

What are some things that a good wine tour guide does/teaches?

A wine tour guide's primary purpose is to ensure their guests' safety while they are also having fun. The point is not to be pedantic. . .a good guide shoves their pride aside. No one is going to lose sleep if they don't hear what the parent varietals of cabernet sauvignon are; however, every-one will remember having fun with their friends and family. Enlightening guests on little known wine trivia, local history, and the culture of the native people is important, but every good tour guide knows when to simply shut up and let their guests enjoy the day so that they look back with great memories.

What are some things that clients should expect, or never do, on a wine tour? (Funny stories accepted).

Please dress appropriately.

Please wear COMFORTABLE shoes. Every winery has concrete floors. Your comfort is what matters!

Please do not chew mint flavored gum/brush your teeth with mint tooth-paste/have mint breath mints for 45 minutes before your tour starts . . .this greatly impacts your taste of the wine!

Please avoid wearing perfume or strongly scented body products, as this affects OTHER people's taste of the wines.

Please eat a hearty breakfast prior to the tour starting . . . it makes your tour (and evening after) so much more enjoyable.

On any wine tour, it is considered "polite" to buy a bottle of wine, per person, per winery, especially at the smallest wineries.

BEER

Callister Brewing Company

Dageraad Brewing

Faculty Brewing Co. and Oddity Kombucha

Parallel 49 Brewing Company

Strathcona Beer Company

R&B Brewing

BRITISH COLUMBIA

● VANCOUVER
● BURNABY

BRITISH COLUMBIA

—

BRITISH COLUMBIA WAS early to the craft scene, and it has trended up ever since—at present, more than 180 breweries are in operation in the territory. Unsurprisingly, the brightest lights on that scene inhabit its signature city, Vancouver, but there are no shortage of worthy spots to visit as you make your way through BC's breathtaking natural beauty.

BRITISH COLUMBIA
BEER
---

*British Columbia's brewers are innovators. They have been since John Mitchell and
Frank Appleton built the Horseshoe Bay Brewery—Canada's first microbrewery—
back in 1982. They are creative entrepreneurs, innovative business owners, who
have nurtured their industry with desire and determination to be the best at what
they do. And they've succeeded. More than 180 breweries dot the super, natural
landscape of BC with new operations opening at an unprecedented rate. Adding
to that, BC brewers win about one-third of all annual Canadian brewing awards
despite the province having less than 20 percent of the country's breweries and less
than 15 percent of the national population.*
–The BC Ale Trail

As recently as the early 1980s, there were no craft breweries in Canada. Just three producers dominated the market: Labatt, Molson, and Carling O'Keefe. Their products were considered unremarkable and similar to each other. Already limited by choice, there were many spans during which no beer was even available in BC due to worker strikes. "Clearly," writes Joe Wiebe, "the beer industry was in need of a major upheaval—perhaps even a revolution."

John Mitchell was a British expat who arrived in Canada in 1954. For the next decades he would work as the bar manager of the Sylvia Hotel in Vancouver and co-owner of Troller Pub in Horseshoe Bay. Fed up with the supply disruptions caused by the strikes, he decided to brew his own beer - something he had never done before and knew nothing about. He reached out to Frank Appleton, a writer who had published a guide for building home breweries, and asked for help. Frank obliged, and they applied to the Liquor Distribution Board to open a new brewing operation. The board's minister, Peter Hyndman, frustrated by the strikes and what he viewed as price fixing by the Big Three breweries, granted Mitchell's application live, during a press conference. "Now they had to do it," writes Wiebe.

Frank and John assembled a makeshift system from repurposed dairy equipment, and Horseshoe Bay Brewing was established, producing just one beer (Bay Ale) exclusively for the Troller Pub. The brewing company did not last long, but it cemented its role in history as Canada's first microbrewery. Appleton left BC in demand as a brewing consultant, integral in launching iconic brands like Deschutes, Ninkasi, Yaletown Brewing, and Nelson Brewing. Mitchell would stay in the area, teaming up with architect Paul Hadfield to create another first for Canada: the brewpub. BC had laws similar to those of its southern neighbors, disallowing the retail sale of beer at the location in which it was brewed. Paul and John lobbied to have the law changed, and were quickly rewarded. Victoria was now home to the Canadian brewpub, Spinnakers.

That same year, two other breweries were put in motion: Granville Island Brewing in Vancouver and Island Pacific Brewing in Saanichton, near Victoria (IPB eventually changed its name to Vancouver Island Brewing). Shaftebury Brewing, Wilson Brewing, Nelson Brewing, and Swans Brewpub would follow suit in the early 1990s. By 2000, there were 25 craft breweries in BC alone. The emergence of bottle shops allowed small producers to avoid the high minimum

requirements of the state-run liquor stores, exposing more Canadians to local microbrews. The emergence of the PNW's beer industry in the United States at the same time inspired the Northerners to elevate their craft.

By 2012, about 50 breweries called BC home. At that same time, Wiebe's popular book, *Craft Beer Revolution: The Insider's Guide to B.C. Breweries* "opened the floodgates," he recalls. "Over the next five years, more than a hundred new breweries would open—an average of 20 new breweries every year! The industry expanded from a respectable 50 breweries in 2013 to more than 150 in what almost seemed like the blink of an eye." Serendipitously, the BC government passed legislation allowing breweries to operate their own tasting rooms (a privilege the local wineries had enjoyed for some time). No longer restricted only to selling kegs to restaurants and bars, the producers could sell their own stuff on tap by the pint and growlers, fueling exponential growth and profit.

"All in all," writes Wiebe, "the future continues to look bright for craft beer in BC I've been saying the same thing for years now, but this mantra remains true today: there has never been a better time to drink beer in British Columbia. Cheers!"

Callister Brewing Company

Vancouver, British Columbia

The Yeast Van neighborhood runs from Powell Street to Commercial Drive, a "rough around the edges" industrial area near the port. The name is a play on words, noting the thriving craft beer culture here on the east side of Vancouver. Storm Brewing was the first brewery here in the 1990s; the area now boasts nearly two dozen. Callister Brewing, however, was the first of its kind in Canada: a collaborative workspace.

Diana McKenzie launched Callister in 2013 to host amateur beer makers in a "brewery incubator" until they became established. They worked on ten such projects until 2020, when they claimed the space as their own and now produce everything themselves. Co-founder and head brewer Chris Lay joined the program after creating an award-winning porter homebrew himself. The brewery is named after neighboring Callister Park, at which Chris's grandfather, Ed, was caretaker, residing under the stands.

Callister is the smallest brewery in Vancouver, but uniquely they have their own series of craft sodas for cocktails. Taproom guests can enjoy 12 rotating beers and guest ciders, and they can also order local gin and vodka mixed with choices like raspberry Earl Grey, ginger beer, hibiscus lemonade, cream soda, and tonic. The patio is perfect for families (including dogs), and guests are welcome to bring their own food to enjoy.

The Yeast District producers work in collaboration with the BC Ale Trail, West Coast Food, and TransLink to provide a safe and easy program for visitors. They provide all the info you need to visit every brewery and enjoy the best local restaurants, all via public transportation. Leave the car at the hotel and snag one of their "Tasting Passports" before getting on the bus. Breweries will "stamp" your passports for drawings and prizes.

Products:

- Hastings Sunrise Wheat Ale—hazy, fruity ale with orange zest

- Playa Lager—craft lager with golden straw color

- Cuban Taxi Guava Gose—2022 Canada Beer Cup Gold Medal winner

- Tin Top Amber Ale—malt-forward red with caramel notes

- Short & Stout Irish Dry Stout—deep, dark, and roasty

- Poptop Grapefruit IPA—West Coast–style with peeled grapefruit

- Fruit Sour—kettle sour of seasonal fruits

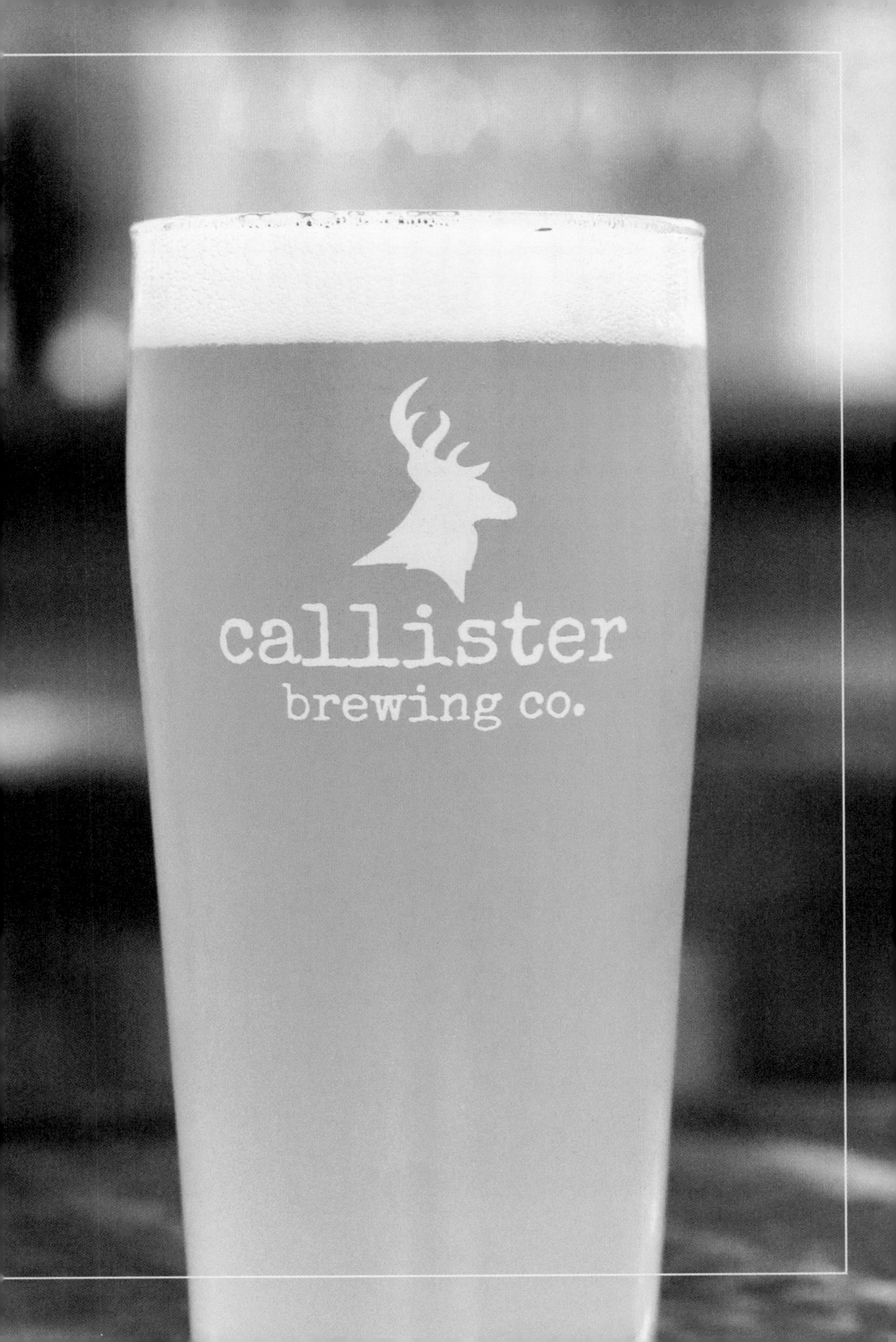
callister
brewing co.

DAGERAAD

Dageraad Brewing

Burnaby, British Columbia

Dageraad Brewing is named after the Dageraadplaats, a neighborhood square on the east side of Antwerp, Belgium. The brewery is our effort to transport a small piece of the beer culture I found in that square home to British Columbia.
—Ben Coli, Founder

Dageraad Brewing is all about bringing the love of Belgian beer culture to British Columbia. Ben Coli discovered his love for the country and its brews early on. "It started off as a summer fling," he says, "but it gradually grew into a passion." After attending brewery school, Ben began taking "beer sabbaticals" to Belgium to learn the craft. He launched the small-batch, artisan brewery in 2014, and by 2018, the Canadian Brewing Awards named it Brewery of the Year. He is quick to note, however, that Dageraad is not Belgian, but rather "Burnabarian." "The beers are Belgian inspired, because those are the beers I like best. If I need any supplemental obsession I won't have to look any farther than Vancouver's vigorous, inventive, and unruly homebrewing community.

"Those first encounters with Belgian beers led me to try to brew them myself at home. Gamblers talk about beginners' luck, because people who are unlucky their first time don't continue gambling. It's the same with brewing. My first Belgian-style homebrew was incredible—fruity, spicy, complex, but light and drinkable. I was hooked.

"Interest grew into obsession, and I began a period of intensive

study. I crisscrossed the country, visiting breweries in tiny Flemish villages and in abbeys in the Ardennes. I picked Belgian brewers' brains to discover what made their beer so amazing. And I returned to the Dageraadplaats again and again.

"Now, after years of study, setbacks, and hard work, we have Dageraad Brewing. The brewery isn't much to look at; just a handful of brewers reveling in their modest collection of stainless steel tanks in a warehouse in Burnaby. But there's something I learned during my visits to Belgian breweries: it doesn't take grandeur in a brewery to make magic in a bottle."

Before visiting their 50-seat tasting room, you can consider their fantastic how-to guide for pouring, tasting, and enjoying their products on their website.

Products:

- Daybreak IPA—fruit-forward, yet balanced, juicy but with a clean finish—refined, even-tempered, and a little nerdy

- White—Belgian-style witbier with a twist: a sprinkle of peppery grains of paradise and a pinch of sumac for a bright, citrusy aroma

- Dagerlager—true crispy boi, with a herbal aroma of noble hops and a firm base of subtly nutty German pilsner malt

- Burnabarian—a table beer, or Belgian-style session ale, lightly spiced with coriander and brewed with oats for a silky mouthfeel

- Brune—a take on a classic Belgian abbey dubbel, combining the mission figs once grown by Franciscan monks with the yeast used by Trappist monks

- Lekkers—a dark ale brewed with chocolate malt, caramelized sugar, and orange peel

- Rainshine—a sunny blonde ale brewed with Citra hops and grapefruit peel

- Irresolution—the brewery's annual tradition of making a beer with all of the leftover hops, Irresolution is different every year, but it's always designed to brighten the holidays

Faculty Brewing Co. and Oddity Kombucha

Vancouver, British Columbia

Husband and wife team Mauricio (the brewer) and Alicia (the architect who designed the brewery) launched Faculty Brewing as an open-source model of sorts, like a college or university (Mauricio was formerly a professor). Recipes are shared (you can find them on the sides of their canned beers), new ideas and innovation are encouraged, and collaboration is a must. "We have nothing to hide," is their motto.

They implement multiple sustainable practices in their production and bottling processes. Water conservation is a focus, all packaging is either recyclable or compostable, and they even utilize their spent grains in baking the cookies they sell.

Their 30-seat taproom is located at their seven-barrel brewery in Vancouver. Guests can have a pint, fill growlers, and grab kegs. Outside food is welcomed. Thursdays are great for stopping by - they feature a weekly new experimental beer, with a portion of sales donated to charity. New visitors will find their beers accessible, as they even label them like classes for incoming freshman:

Our beers are numbered using a system based on the way in which universities and colleges number courses by their degree of complexity and expertise. Each beer's corresponding number reflects the sophistication of its flavor profile. Lower numbers indicate a more entry-level beer, while higher numbers are reserved for more experimental and bold-flavored beers.

Products:

- 123 Sourveza—a fusion of styles: inspired by both a classic Mexican light lager, and a citrus-forward kettle sour

- 165 Shower Beer—light and easy-drinking qualities while also offering a fruit basket of aromas from the heavily dry hop of Callista and Cashmere

- 231 Black Currant Ale—an intensely red-purple hue, with a grape-candy-like aroma and a tart finish

- 250 London Fog Ale—smooth, easy-drinking ale infused with Silk Road's London Fog organic black tea blend; bergamot, vanilla, and spice complement a creamy mouthfeel

- 257 Sakura Saison—pilsner malt and flaked corn create a super light base layered with a touch of hibiscus for an iconic pink blush

- 299 Turmeric Ale—pale ale spiced with cardamom and coriander

- 445 Galaxy IPA—brewed with malted wheat and oats; full-bodied, silky-smooth experience, plus an expressive English yeast strain amplifies all of those wonderfully tropical aromas and flavors

- 710 Oaked Stout—aromas of vanilla from American oak complement the roasted malt character of this delicious dry stout

Parallel 49 Brewing Company

Vancouver, British Columbia

 *In 2012, friends Anthony Frustagli, Nick Paladino, and Mike Sleeman quit their cushy day jobs to go all in on a shared dream of opening their very own craft brewery. Although bursting with ambition and excitement, the founding trio needed a technical lead to bring their ideas to life. Enter Graham With, a highly respected and well-known Vancouver homebrewer perfect for the position. Friend Michael Tod handled the sales, bringing diehard craft beer enthusiast Scott Venema along with him. And just like that, Parallel 49 Brewing Company had its first six investors—and its first six employees. Today, Parallel 49 Brewing is sold in over 100 cities across Canada, serving up more than 70 unique brews per year. With over 90 employees, P49's next step is to move farther into Eastern Canada while continuing to deliver on their mission statement: Making great beer accessible to all!*

Strathcona Beer Company
Vancouver, British Columbia

Tim Knight and his posse of friends are the driving force behind Strathcona Beer Company, located in Vancouver's oldest residential neighborhood. Tim has strong ties to the community as both president of the 25-hectoliter brewery and the operator of his family's general contracting business, responsible for the construction of many nearby building projects. Their 67-seat taproom, opened in 2016, serves as a collaborative community space for gathering and sipping their IPAs, fruit beers, radlers, and seasonals. They have indoor and outdoor seating and offer gourmet pizzas and canned beer to go.

Products:

- Premium Pilsner—complex rich pale Czech lager, with considerable malt and hop character; well balanced with a long, rounded finish

- Beach Lemon Mandarin Radler—a precise blend of lemon peel, fresh mandarin juice, and beer with a tart, clean finish

- Strath Lager—a premium American-style lager with pilsner malts, Munich, and flaked corn, lightly hopped with Hallertau Mittelfruh and Lemondrop

- Beautiful Pale Ale—light, refreshing pale ale with a base of Pilsner malts, hopped with Mosaic, Simcoe, and Amarillo hops

- Love Buzz Lemon Coconut Cupcake Sour—lemon juice, toasted coconut flakes, and a touch of lactose and brown sugar; light in body with a tart finish

- Big Sexy Funk IPA—a dry, hazy IPA that is beautifully aromatic with big citrus accents and fresh tropical fruit notes

R&B Brewing

Vancouver, British Columbia

R&B is one of Vancouver's original microbreweries, located just off main street in the city's Brewery Creek district.

You'll hear an eclectic mix of rock, R&B, and worldly music blasting out our doors as you take in the sweet smell of boiling wort and the grinding roar of our mill. Emblematic of who we are, and where we live.

Their taproom is kid and dog-friendly, offering visitors a vegan-friendly menu of pizzas, sandwiches, salads, and snacks alongside their popular brews.

Products:

- Stolen Bike Lager—crisp, golden, traditional

- Vancouver Special IPA—resinous, candied orange, guava

- Hipster Haze Hazy IPA—pineapple, tangerine, papaya

- Free the Triple—Belgian triple, dry-hopped with Amarillo

- Saucerful of Secrets Pale Ale—ingle-hop brewed pale ale; brewed with Vic Secret

- Raven Cream Ale—chocolate, coffee, smooth

PHOTOGRAPHY CREDITS

—

Pages 38, 39, and 40–41 courtesy of Deschutes Brewery. Page 43 courtesy of Ale Apothecary. Pages 46, 47, 48, and 49 courtesy of Crux Fermentation Project. Pages 50, 51, and 52 courtesy of Bevel Craft Brewing. Pages 53 and 54 courtesy of Ninkasi Brewing. Page 55 courtesy of ColdFire Brewing. Pages 57 and 58 courtesy of Ecliptic Brewing. Pages 59, 60, and 61 courtesy of Great Notion. Pages 67, 68, and 69 courtesy of Reverend Nat's Hard Cider. Pages 71 and 72 courtesy of Legend Cider Company. Page 79 courtesy of King Estate Winery. Pages 80, 81, 82–83, 84, and 85 courtesy of Abacela Winery. Pages 87 and 88 courtesy of Ewing Young Distillery. Page 91 courtesy of Freeland Spirits. Page 92 courtesy of Hood River Distillers. Page 97 courtesy of Ransom Spirits. Page 107 courtesy of Fremont Brewing. Pages 109 and 112 courtesy of Georgetown Brewing Co. Pages 114, 115, and 116 courtesy of Locust Cider. Pages 117, 120, and 121 courtesy of Incline Cider Company. Pages 126–127, 128, 129, 130, 131, and 132 courtesy of Chateau Ste. Michelle Winery. Pages 134–135, 145, 151, 152 (top), and 157 (top) courtesy of Andrea Johnson Photography. Page 144 courtesy of Greg Lehman. Pages 146–147 courtesy of Bionic Wines. Page 148 courtesy of Bob Holmes. Page 150 courtesy of Horsepower Vineyards. Page 151 (bottom), 153, and 154–155 courtesy of Hors Catégorie Vineyards. Page 156 courtesy of No Girls Wines. Page 157 (bottom) courtesy of Tyson Kopfer. Pages 159, 160, and 161 courtesy of OOLA. Pages 162 and 165 courtesy of Copperworks Distilling Company. Pages 166, 167, and 168 courtesy of Black Rock Spirits. Pages 170 and 172 courtesy of Demitri Pallis. Pages 173 and 175 courtesy of Dry Fly Distilling. Pages 176 and 177 courtesy of Unicorn Distillery. Page 185 courtesy of Alliteration Ales. Pages 186, 187, and 188 courtesy of Lost Grove Brewing. Pages 190 and 191 courtesy of Sockeye Brewing. Page 193 courtesy of Chalice Brewing. Pages 200 and 201 courtesy of Lone Mountain Farms & Brewery. Pages 208 and 209 courtesy of Par Terre Winery. Pages 210 and 212 courtesy of Hat Ranch Winery. Pages 214 and 215 courtesy of Telaya Wine Co. Pages 220 and 223 courtesy of Clearwater Canyon Cellars. Pages 221 and 222 courtesy of Brad Stinson. Pages 225 and 226 courtesy of Huston Vineyards. Pages 227, 228, and 229 courtesy of Rivaura Estate Vineyard and Winery. Pages 240, 241, 242, and 243 courtesy of Callister Brewing Company. Pages 244, 245, 246, and 247 courtesy of Dageraad Brewing. Page 253 courtesy of R&B Brewing. All other photos used under official license from Shutterstock and Adobe Stock.

DEDICATION

In memory of Murray Stenson—the best to ever do it.

ABOUT THE AUTHOR

—

Neil Ratliff is the owner/operator of Emerald City Cocktails, the largest professional bartending service on the west coast. A native of Orlando, Florida, he moved to Seattle in 2012 to complete his master's degree at the University of Washington and, after graduating, decided to remain in Seattle's thriving bar and cocktail scene and make the city his new home.

A two-decade veteran of the bar scene, Neil has been slinging drinks at bars and events in Orlando and Seattle since the law said he could. He earned his chops through TGI Fridays' exceptional bar training program, and after years of high-volume experience he joined the opening team of Vintage Ultra Lounge and Ceviche Tapas Bar in Downtown Orlando. To pay his way through graduate school, he crafted cocktails in Seattle's fine dining circuit until launching Emerald City Cocktails in 2016. He is also the author of *Seattle Cocktails*.

About Cider Mill Press Book Publishers

Good ideas ripen with time. From seed to harvest, Cider Mill Press brings fine reading, information, and entertainment together between the covers of its creatively crafted books. Our Cider Mill bears fruit twice a year, publishing a new crop of titles each spring and fall.

"Where Good Books Are Ready for Press"

501 Nelson Place
Nashville, Tennessee 37214

cidermillpress.com